Sound is your superpower

Discovering, developing, maintaining and maximising your skills

Thanks, and acknowledgements

Very many thanks to my colleagues and friends who took the time to check the text of this book and offer their opinions. Writing a book which is accessible and comprehensible is a serious challenge and without such support it is impossible.

© Charlotte Davies, 2023

Published by Fit-2-Learn CIC

All rights reserved. No part of this book may be reproduced, adapted, stored in a retrieval system or transmitted by any means, electronic, mechanical, photocopying, or otherwise without the prior written permission of the author.

The rights of Charlotte Davies to be identified as the author of this work have been asserted in accordance with the Copyright, Designs and Patents Act 1988.

A CIP catalogue record for this book is available from the British Library.

ISBN 978-1-5262-0985-6

Book layout and design by Clare Brayshaw

Prepared and printed by:

York Publishing Services Ltd
64 Hallfield Road
Layerthorpe
York YO31 7ZQ

Tel: 01904 431213

Website: www.yps-publishing.co.uk

Contents

Key to icons used in this book

Interesting facts are highlighted with this icon.

Opportunities and ideas to experiment with sound are highlighted with this icon.

Alarm bells should ring if a person is having difficulty undertaking certain sound processing activities.

Ideas to improve sound processing skills.

Background of Fit 2 Learn CIC

Fit 2 Learn CIC work with Tomatis sound therapy technology and methods in order to bring our clients to the state where their motor skills, sound processing and visual processing all work together coherently, so that they can learn calmly and efficiently. This stage of development is called "**motor-sensory integration**". Everyone should aim to achieve this and maintain it for life.

Initially, when the company was set up, the idea had been to support struggling school children. Then we found that many people of all ages had gaps in their motor-sensory integration which they wished to resolve. When they addressed those gaps, then they experienced much calmer, more productive lives.

Central to our work and moving all the senses and motor skills is Tomatis sound therapy. The Tomatis website is www.tomatis.com

The Fit 2 Learn website is www.fit-2-learn.com where you can find links to various resources to support other areas of development beyond sound processing.

The Fit 2 Learn programme is outlined in the diagram below. All humans should progress through these stages of development in order to be efficient learners. Very few people can naturally easily learn everything, therefore it is a useful framework for us all to work on ways in which we can fine-tune our physical and cognitive skills.

Humans have evolved to develop outside the womb and in stages. Each stage needs to be mastered in order to create a secure foundation for the next stage.

Humans are essentially hunter-gatherers and have evolved to move widely. Modern environments do not support good human development. Therefore, we need to proactively support every person to develop fully and properly and maintain good development for life.

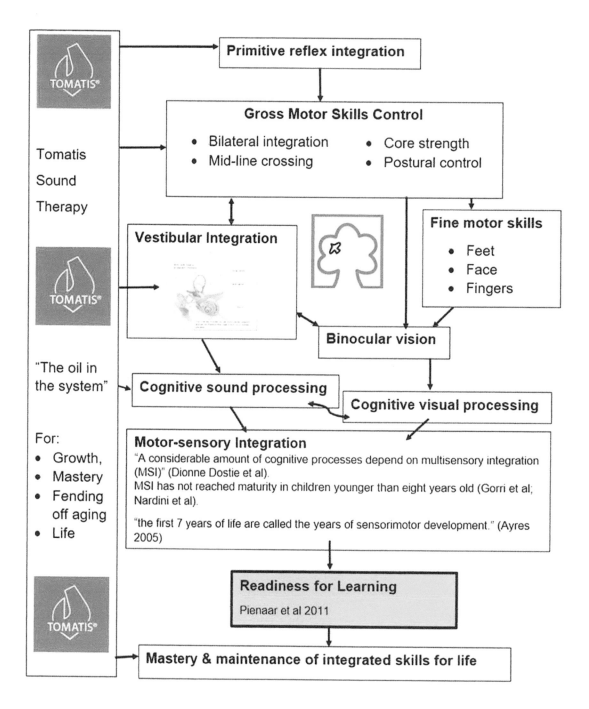

Sound is the oil in the whole system.

How to use this book

This book seeks to get sound processing and hearing out of the box, to explore its amazing power and to make sound processing easier to understand and manage for the typical person.

Understanding how sound works is significantly improved if a person engages in the process of consciously thinking about sound. Therefore, the book is designed with many practical activities to fully understand sound.

The book is laid out so that you can dip in and out to parts that interest you and build understanding. It is a book that can be read alone or be explored by communities and family groups engaging together in the activities.

It is intended to be fun and informative – enjoy!

1

What is sound processing?

The physics of sound

Human perception of sound

Music and reading – what happens in the brain?

What is sound processing?

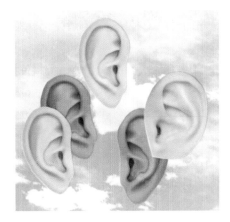

Sound processing is vastly more than just hearing.

Sound processing is an active function in a living human.

It is the ability to make sense of all the sounds in the world around us. That is:

- How the brain works with the body to make sense of sounds as an input.
- As an output in terms of speech, singing and producing sounds of all kinds from foreign languages to playing musical instruments.
- Our body works with left and right sides of body and ears to make sense of the sounds that come to us. Ideally we can:
  - Make sense of even the quietest of sounds.
  - Tell the direction of sound and whether it is moving.
  - Understand sound in context.
  - Understand every syllable of speech and language.
  - Sense a person's emotions from the tone of their speech.
  - Sing in tune.
  - Learn foreign languages.
  - Remember what someone has said.
  - Hear speech in noisy environments and block out irrelevant sounds.
  - Respond rapidly to auditory warnings.

Unfortunately, the skill of sound processing is very rarely checked or supported to develop fully.

You can take control of your own sound processing skills and understand how to develop and maintain them for life.

The physics of sound

Sound comes to us from all directions. It moves in waves.

Our bodies are molecules of water and solids and the sound waves impact on our whole bodies.

Sound that is perceptible by humans has frequencies from around 20 hertz to 20,000 hertz. (Hertz is abbreviated to Hz.)

20Hz are very deep sounds and 20,000Hz are very high-pitched sounds. As we age we tend to lose very high-pitched sounds first.

Explore the keys on a piano from low to high.

The white keys on the piano are A, B, C, D, E, F and G; the black keys are called sharps or flats: We use the sharp ♯ and flat ♭ symbols, along with the letters, to designate the sounds on the black keys. The sharp raises the note by one semitone (the smallest musical interval), while the flat lowers it by one semitone. The black key between C and D can be called C# or D♭. Notes with these two names have the same pitch. Other examples are: A#=B♭, D#=E♭, F#=G♭, G#=A♭.

The key on the far left is A0 which has a pitch of 27.5Hz. The key on the far right is C8, it has a pitch of 4186Hz.

If you play every A key on the piano you will move in a pattern of hertz that doubles: 27.5Hz; 55Hz; 110Hz; 220Hz; 440Hz; 880Hz; 1760Hz; 3520Hz.

Play all the A keys and consider how they sound different from each other and from other notes.

In air at standard temperature and pressure, the wavelengths of sound waves range from 17m to 17mm. The more intense a sound the higher the sound waves. Think about the difference between the sound of a pin dropping and the sound of a rocket launch.

A big vibration causes large sound waves that carry a lot of energy e.g., a balloon popping has this shape.

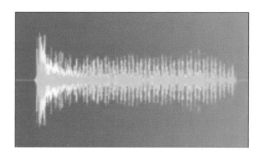

Sound waves have two key elements: pressure and time. These fundamental elements form the basis of all sound waves. They can be used to describe every sound we hear.

This is a little owl hooting.

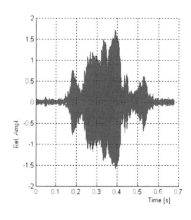

Explore: search online for sound waves of different things around you.

Possible terms to search under might include:

- Sound wave images
- Voice sound wave images
- The science of sound waves images
- Sound waves of cats purring
- Sound waves of explosions
- Sound waves of bird song

Compare and discuss the different waves that you see and try to understand the shape of the waves from different sound sources.

Sound is transmitted through gases, materials and liquids as longitudinal waves. As the source continues to vibrate the medium e.g., the air, the vibrations move away from the source at the speed of sound, thus forming the sound wave.

The movement of molecules by the sound

Sound source

Wavelength

The speed of sound depends on the medium the waves pass through. Sound moves slowest through gasses and fastest through solids.

The speed of sound changes with conditions such as temperature and altitude.

In 20°C (68°F) air at sea level, the speed of sound is approximately 343m/s

In fresh water the speed of sound is approximately 1482m/s

Through muscles the speed of sound is approximately 1575m/s

Through bones the speed of sound is approximately 4080m/s

In steel, the speed of sound is about 5960m/s

Experiment: Feel how sounds move through different mediums.

- Lie in the bath or go to a swimming pool and consciously think about sound movement above and below water.
- If you place a small speaker playing music (e.g., your mobile phone) on your coccyx or sternum you should be able to feel sound waves coming through your bones. (Remember to take the device out of any protective coverings to get maximum effect.)
- Take a thick metal pan, place your speaker in the pan, hold everything in place and hold the pan to your ear. Then take the metal pan away. Feel the difference between a sound coming through metal and a sound coming through air.

Put the speaker in the bottom of the pan so that the sound is directed into the metal. Listen on the other side of the pan.

- As you go through life consider how different things sound. Things like doors closing, people speaking, dogs barking, doorbells ringing. Think about what their sound waves might look like. Is there a lot of energy or little energy? Closing a door quietly, versus slamming a door should give a very good contrast. How long do the sound waves last?

Sound reverberates

Sound bounces off surfaces like walls and repeats the original sound in a weaker form, these are reverberations. Multiple repetitions of the original sound can make it difficult to process the sound.

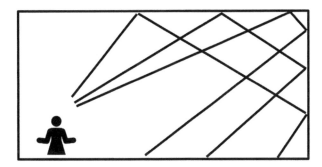

Some public address systems can also cause problems with conveying sound because they create a slight delay on the sound projection. That again reverberates and creates feedback which makes processing the sound exhausting.

If you really want people to process sound comfortably in a space, it is worth taking the time to make sure that the room and the technology work.

Some buildings are very well designed and can make sound dramatic and glorious. Which is very exciting for many people, unless they struggle to process sound, in which case it might come across as chaotic and threatening or overwhelming.

The online magazine *The Spaces* listed the following ten buildings and constructions as interesting acoustic spaces. (https://thespaces.com/10-buildings-with-extraordinary-acoustics/)

- Tvísöngur, Iceland
- Forest megaphones, Estonia
- Fertőrákos Cave Theatre, Hungary
- The Music Hall at the Āli Qapu Palace, Iran
- Denge sound mirrors, UK
- The Danish Music Museum, Denmark
- Brunel Museum, UK
- Ekko, Denmark
- The Whispering Gallery at St Paul's Cathedral, UK
- Prenzlauer Berg water tower and tanks, Berlin

It is possible to visit these spaces online, but to fully feel how sound works in these spaces, find time to visit some of them or similar buildings.

How we experience and process sound therefore depends on environment. Like all apes we are adapted for living in the air outside in the open. Which explains why many people feel better when they go outside.

It is possible to design spaces so that sound is absorbed, and reverberation is minimised. Hard surfaces like glass panels and hard floors increase reverberation, whereas soft furnishings absorb the sound.

Some humans, usually blind ones, have developed echolocation i.e., the ability to navigate using sound. Their heightened sense of sound is used to feel the reverberations coming off surfaces around them. Daniel Kish explains how he does this in this video https://www.youtube.com/watch?v=uHoaihGWB8U&ab_channel=TED

Meredith Monk used a tower (Ann Hamilton's Tower, Oct 2008) as a musical instrument with human voices and instruments to create an interesting piece of music, entitled "Songs of Ascension". https://www.youtube.com/watch?v=c3mSVR3xtfU&list=RDc3mSVR3xtfU&start_radio=1&rv=c3mSVR3xtfU&t=7&ab_channel=mmonkhouse

Explore the acoustics and reverberations in buildings and structures in your local area. Churches, tunnels and railway arches are often good starting points. Keep a video diary of your experiences.

Seeing pattern in sounds

It is possible to see sound patterns through subjecting matter such as sand, or liquids to music, this is called cymatics. A surface is vibrated, and regions of maximum and minimum displacement are made visible in a thin coating of particles, paste or liquid. Different patterns emerge depending on the geometry of the plate and the driving frequency. Nigel Stanford has made various videos of this phenomenon.

https://nigelstanford.com/Cymatics/?s=youtube&p=ferro

Cymatics: Speaker Dish
Nigel John Stanf...
622K subscribers
Subscribed
5.5K
Share

Cymatics: Ferrofluid
Nigel John Stanf...
622K subscribers
Subscribed
4K
Share

You can repeat such experiments at home.

In space there is no sound. Sound travels through the vibration of atoms and molecules in a medium such as air. In space there is no air, so sound has no way to travel.

Human perception of sound

In earth's <u>atmosphere</u>, engines, <u>water</u>, fire, rain, wind, earthquake, animals and so on produce their own unique sounds. Which we learn to recognise as we grow.

An auditory stimulus takes only 8–10ms to reach the human brain, by comparison a visual stimulus takes 20–40ms. Sound processing is a human's first alarm system. We can respond to sounds faster than we are conscious of, which is essential if we are escaping a threat, and this has been useful to mankind for its survival.

Humans create sounds through speech and other activities, such as clapping their hands and stamping their feet.

Rhythm is an important part of every human's experience of life, it is embedded in the basic functioning of their own heart rate and breathing. Humans will unconsciously synchronise their body rhythms with those around them. This is an important part of survival and feeling safe. Singing and dancing together are all part of being human and in-tune with each other.

Age	Normal heart rates Beats per minute resting	Normal respiration rates Breaths pre minute resting
premature	120–170	40–70
0–3 months	100–150	35–55
3–6 months	90–120	30–45
6–12 months	80–120	25–40
1–3 years	70–110	20–30
3–6 years	65–110	20–25
6–12 years	60–95	14–22
Over 12 years	55–85	12–18

Research by Professor Usha Goshwami has identified that learning to speak starts with rhythm. Infants experience rhythm pre- and post-birth, from their mother's body, from singing, from rhythmic movement such as cradling and so on. Thus, the child learns the basic rhythmic patterns of their own language.

Humans have developed culture and technology, such as music, telephone and radio that allows them to generate, record, transmit and broadcast sound. Even the most primitive tribes will make music and humans are believed to have been making music since palaeolithic times (3.3 million years ago to approximately 11,650 years ago).

Being in-tune with each other is an important aspect of being human. Humans are social animals who benefit from cooperating together. Much learning and social adaptation happens outside the womb in humans. Cultural knowledge has to be passed down inter-generationally to quickly access the accumulated knowledge of the community.

Humans can synchronise their body rhythms by engaging in activities such as singing and dancing together, or breathing slowly and rhythmically, or even playing a game together such as playing "peepo". All human cultures have some form of the game "peepo" that they play with infants and recent neural research has shown that such interaction with infants promotes brain growth.

Being in-tune is also important for group safety and sense of security. However, a person who is habitually anxious can unconsciously cause the whole group to become anxious. It is therefore important that people actively work on maintaining calm coherent breathing and heart rates. See page 40 for strategies to achieve this.

Human Perception of sound

How humans perceive and make sense of sound has a vocabulary of its own.

- **Noise** is an unwanted sound.

- **Rhythm** is a regular repeated pattern of sound.

- **Direction** of sound: both ears help determine the direction sound comes from. There is a time lag to each ear, the wavelength and tone of the sound are all important factors for the brain when determining the direction of sound.

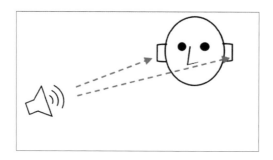

- **Pitch** is perceived as how "low" or "high" a sound is and represents the cyclic, repetitive nature of the vibrations that make up sound. The pitch can be represented in hertz e.g., 125Hz is a low-pitched whereas 8000Hz is a high-pitched sound.

- **Duration** is perceived as how "long" or "short" a sound is and relates to onset and offset signals created by nerve responses to sounds.

- **Loudness** is perceived as how "loud" or "soft" a sound is and relates to the totalled number of auditory nerve stimulations over short cyclic time periods. Loudness is measured in decibels.

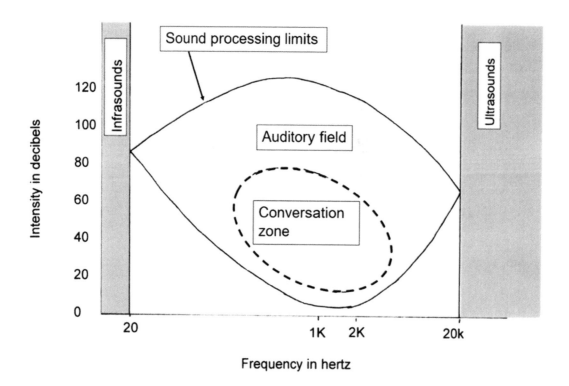

The human ear has a dynamic range from 0dB (threshold) to 120–130dB in the middle frequency range (1–2 kHz). For lower or higher frequencies, the range is narrowed. However, all sounds above 90dB are damaging to the inner ear and can even do irreversible damage above 120dB.

- **Timbre** is perceived as the quality of different sounds (e.g., the thud of a falling rock, the whir of a drill, the tone of a musical instrument or the quality of a voice) and represents the preconscious allocation of a sonic identity to a sound e.g., "It's a dog!".

- **Sonic texture** refers to the number of sound sources and the interaction between them. The word *texture*, in this context, relates to the cognitive separation of auditory objects whether in a café or a piece of music. In music, texture is often referred to as the difference between:

(a) unison is when all sources of sound emit at the same time at the same pitch. Crowds can also speak in unison or dogs can bark in unison. Many voices or sounds are working together. Gregorian chant is monophonic – i.e., everyone is making the same sound at the same time.

(b) polyphony is when there are two or more voices or sound sources at the same time producing simultaneous lines of independent melody. Rounds, canons and fugues are all examples of polyphonic music. There are many recordings of songs such as "Frère Jacques" sung in the round on YouTube.

(c) homophony is when one sound or line of melody is being played by multiple instruments and voices at the same time. There is one main melody and accompanying harmony. This is useful when the words need to be understood. Scott Joplin's "Maple Leaf Rag" is homophonic music.

Sonic texture can also relate to, for example, the sounds of a busy cafél; a sound which might be referred to as a "cacophony" – i.e. there is no pattern to the sounds that can be easily detected and you will struggle to focus on a single conversation

Sound processing and perception is unique to every person. Every human hears sound slightly differently.

Experiment: Play games to see how well you and your friends, and family can identify the different aspects of sound.

- Play Chinese Whispers in different environments, from a noisy, busy café, to a large quiet space with good acoustics, to your home environment. Think about what makes it easier or more difficult to pass the message from person to person. Note: Chinese Whispers is a game where a short message is whispered from one person to another, and the last person compares their perception of the message with the first person who sent the message.

- Hide a mobile phone in a room and then get someone to call the phone and observe how easily a person can identify the location of the sound and find the phone.

- Go for a walk and consciously identify sounds and their location.

- Make a pretend giant piano to jump up and down on when the players hear specific notes. Mark out on the floor or on steps the giant piano and play a note on a xylophone or a piano... start with one note until everyone is confident that they can hear the first note, then try two notes and see if people can jump appropriately to the correct step – i.e., they can, without seeing, make sense of the notes.

- Blindfold one player and place a bunch of keys at their feet. Take it in turns to creep up to the blindfolded player to get the keys. Think about how the blindfolded person uses aspects of sound to detect the person creeping towards them. Consider how the person doing the creeping tries to minimise the sounds that they make. Could you change rooms to make the game more or less challenging? Would it be different outside?

- Experiment with a xylophone or drum or an empty tin making long sounds and short sounds; loud sounds and quiet sounds. What do you need to do? What makes a difference?

- Have an auditory quiz identifying the sound from recordings of sounds. There are various examples available on YouTube, such as this one: https://www.youtube.com/watch?v=U-btSLpuybU&ab_channel=MisterTeach

- Experiment with reciting a poem or singing a song in unison and in a round. How easy is it to work together and to keep to your parts? Does it feel good to speak in unison? At what point does complex sound move from joyous to a cacophony that you are not enjoying?

You will soon notice if one member of your group struggles with these activities. Think carefully about what aspects of the activities they are finding hard. Make a note and think about how you can help them understand and develop the skill.

If there is a persistent problem then, please consider consulting a Tomatis Consultant to get to the root of any sound processing problems. www.tomatis.com

Music and reading – what happens in the brain?

Understanding speech in the brain

According to the Geschwind-Wernicke model, when you hear a word spoken, this auditory signal is processed first in your brain's primary auditory cortex (8 – see image below), which then sends it on to the neighbouring Wernicke's area (9). Wernicke's area associates the structure of this signal with the representation of a word stored in your memory, thus enabling you to retrieve the meaning of the particular word.

So, when you hear the word "dog" the sound has to be transmitted via the auditory cortex (8) to the Wernicke's area (9) to match to meaning of the particular word. The left cerebral hemisphere is the dominant side of the brain in most people.

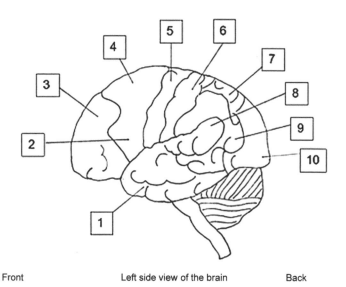

Key: 1 = memory area;
2 = Broca's speech area;
3 = higher mental functions;
4 = premotor function area;
5 = primary motor function area;
6 = Primary sensory area;
7 = angular gyrus;
8 = auditory association area;
9 = Wernicke's area;
10 = Visual area.

Front   Left side view of the brain   Back

By contrast, when you read a word out loud, the information is perceived first by your visual cortex (10), which then transfers it to the angular gyrus (7), from which it is sent on to Wernicke's area (9).

Note: in practice many people do not visually process when they read, but bypass the visual system and send the message via their auditory system. This is a slow method of reading where the word is visually decoded, then spoken out aloud or mouthed and the person auditorily processes the sound. These people tend to have slow reading speeds and/or poor comprehension.

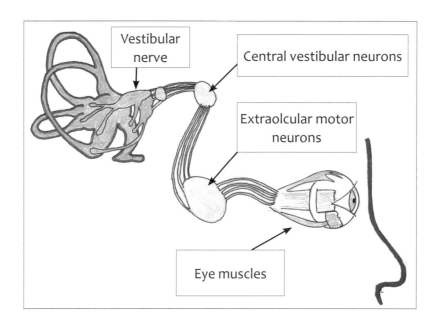

In the Case Studies section it will be possible to see situations where sound and vision do not work together and how that impacts on making sense of reading, writing and puzzles.

However, when a person processes the word, it is Wernicke's area that recognises the word and correctly interprets it according to the context. For you then to pronounce the word yourself, this information must be transmitted to the Broca's area (2), which plans the pronunciation process. Lastly, this information is routed to the motor cortex (5), which controls the muscles that you use to pronounce the word.

Not all neurologists agree with this model of language processing, but most agree that the left hemisphere plays a specific role in identifying the word and that the role of the right hemisphere in understanding the context in which language is used. The right side is important for understanding non-literal language such as sarcasm and irony and for social engagement.

Normally, the language specialisation develops in the left hemisphere, consequently it is advantageous to be right-ear dominant.

The above is just a simplification of what the brain does. In real life when a person hears the word "dog" many areas in the brain might light up which hold associations with the person's experiences to date of dogs.

Some people associate dogs with happy memories, others have had frightening experiences.

You can experience how your brain reacts to individual words by playing word association games. For a word association game, all a person needs to do is to start by saying one word, i.e., the first word that pops into their head. Then the next person says the first word they think of which is associated with the previous word. Take turns back and forth if two people are playing or go around the circle if it is a group.

Understanding and processing music in the brain

Music triggers a wide range of areas in the brain and can trigger a desire to move. This phenomenon is very well outlined in Daniel Levitin's book, *This is Your Brain on Music*.

A simple summary of the areas of the brain affected by music might include:

- The auditory cortex to interpret the music.
- The Wernicke region to comprehend the lyrics of the songs.
- The Broca region to sing along to the music.
- The hippocampus to trigger memories.
- The nucleus accumbens, the amygdala and the cerebellum to give an emotional response.
- The motor cortex to prompt a person to move in time with the music.

Music is a very good emotional and physical stimulus to humans. In the early years it helps develop language skills; and in seniors it helps with memory retrieval. Throughout life music is a useful tool for emotional regulation and creating a sense of joy.

2

Human anatomy of sound processing

Sound and the nervous system

Sound and Porges' long polyvagal theory

Strategies for calming the nervous system

Human anatomy of sound processing

The science of sound processing in brief

This is just intended to be a quick summary to get people to grasp the basics.

The basic anatomy of one ear

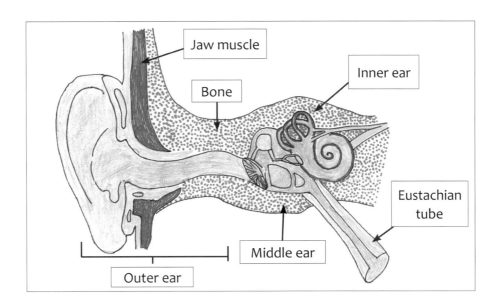

Explore your own ears. Feel them. Feel behind each ear there is a bony lump, inside there is your inner ear, which is why bone conduction of sound works. Clench your jaw and feel movement in your ears. Hum to feel your ears vibrate.

Sound working in stereo

Humans have two ears which must work together. So, everything is happening in stereo.

There is also a dominant ear. This should be the right ear in children over six years of age and adults, except for about 30% of left-handed people for whom it is the left ear. This is because usually speech processing is done by the left-brain hemisphere, so it is quicker for processing if the right ear is dominant.

Humans process sound through air and bone conduction. Both systems must work together coherently.

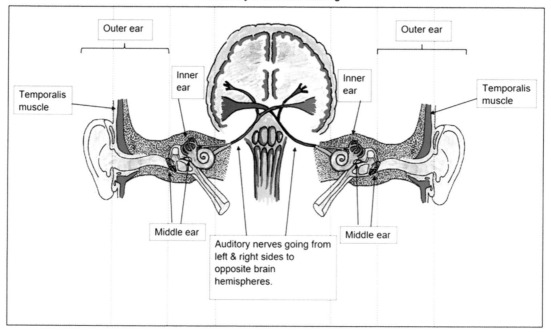

Anatomy of binaural hearing

Both ears must work together efficiently to make good sense of sound, to sends messages to and from the brain. That cannot be assumed. It should be checked and maintained throughout life.

Sound and the brain

Sound processing in a human is linked to eight cranial nerves, that is, nerves linking the brain to the body and sending messages back and forth.

The key point is that sound impacts on global development and wellbeing throughout life. Therefore, like any other skill, we need to check it and maintain it.

Of particular significance is the vestibular system in the inner ear that impacts on motor skills control, including balance and postural control. There are also links between the inner ear and the facial muscles.

Posture and good sound processing skills are linked. It is possible to assume that if a person does not have upright posture their sound processing is compromised in some way. It may be that their sound processing is causing poor posture; or their poor posture is causing problems with sound processing.

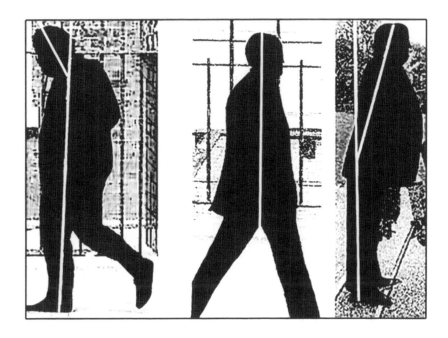

Sound processing can also impact on facial expression if a person is very left- or right-ear dominant. That can cause them to speak off one side of the face or the other.

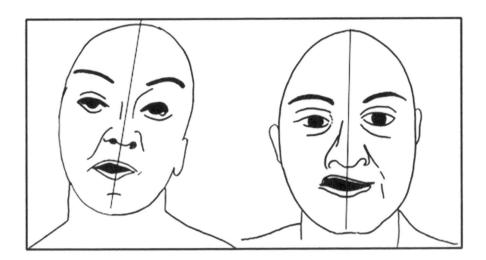

Ideally there is a balance between left and right sides of sound processing. You need both, to balance processing the speech of others, along with all the other aspects of social engagement, such as reading facial expression.

If a person habitually leans off to one side, it may indicate that they have extremely unbalanced sound processing. Balancing the sound processing helps balance the whole person.

Sound and the nervous system

Picture guide to the cranial nerves and sound

Sound processing is connected to eight cranial nerves. This means that an impact on sound can also compromise everything else connected to that nerve. This is really useful for a quick response when a person is under threat. However, as you will see it can produce long-term problems if a person puts inappropriate pressure on some nerves or is trapped in a hyper-alert state.

Cranial nerve V

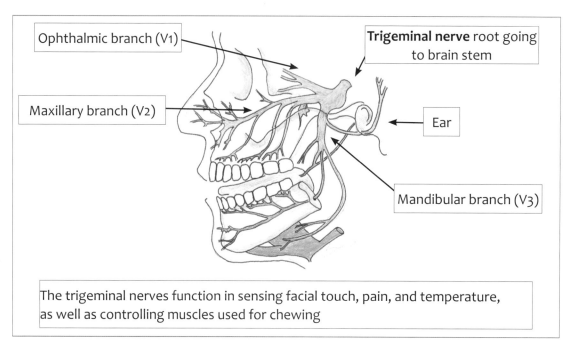

The trigeminal nerves function in sensing facial touch, pain, and temperature, as well as controlling muscles used for chewing

Cranial nerve V shows that:

Sound processing through the middle ears is connected to the eyes, the jaw, the tongue and facial muscles.

Sound is connected to vision and to jaw movements. This is important for reading for meaning. All of the senses need to work together. A problem with one area will have an impact on the others.

A common problem is that many people clench their jaws or grind their teeth. This impacts on sound processing skills via the middle ear. It is an overflow gesture related to poor mid-line crossing skills. This can also manifest in excessive blinking. Steps to overcome this issue are discussed on page 110.

Cranial nerve VII

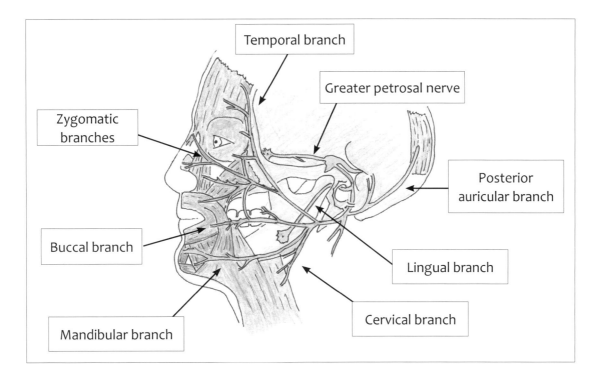

Cranial nerve VII shows that:

Sound processing through the middle ears is connected to the muscles around the eyes, the jaw, the tongue and facial muscles.

These are all areas of your face connected to social engagement. Sound processing, speech and facial muscles work together to make sense of other people's social cues. Also, sound processing and sound production, i.e., speech, work together.

It is also possible to see why inappropriate pressure on nerves can trigger migraines and tinnitus.

Cranial nerve VIII

Cranial nerve VIII shows that:

Sound processing through the inner ears is connected to the vestibular system which controls the sense of movement and balance. The inner ear has a profound impact on movement and motor skills.

The cochlear transmits sound waves at different frequencies to the brain.

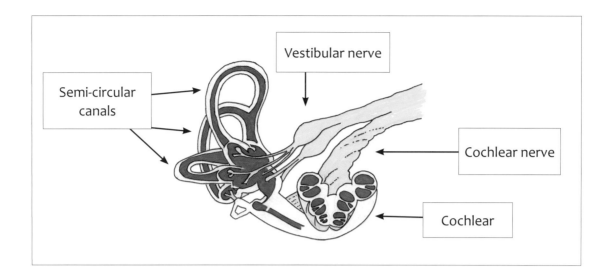

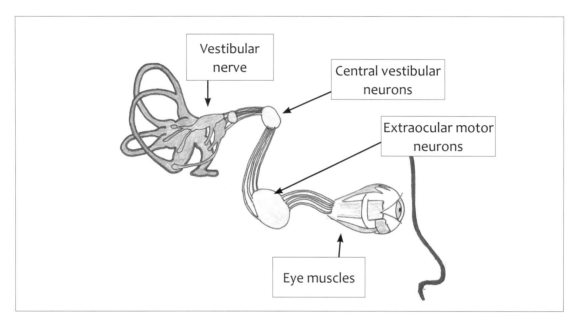

An important part of cranial nerve VIII is that is links sound and vision. That helps humans understand and process everything from where they are in space, to numeracy and literacy.

Disruption to sound or vision will impact on the other system. Humans hear to see and see to hear.

Cranial nerve IX

Cranial nerve IX shows that:

Sound processing through the middle ears is connected to the vagus nerve. Also, it links larynx and pharynx especially during speaking and swallowing. Tongue, tonsils and saliva glands are also connected.

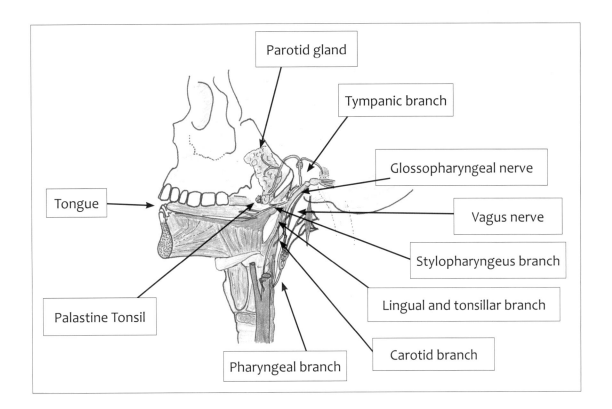

 Consider how, when a person is anxious, the mouth goes dry, the throat tightens and there is a feeling of not being able to speak.

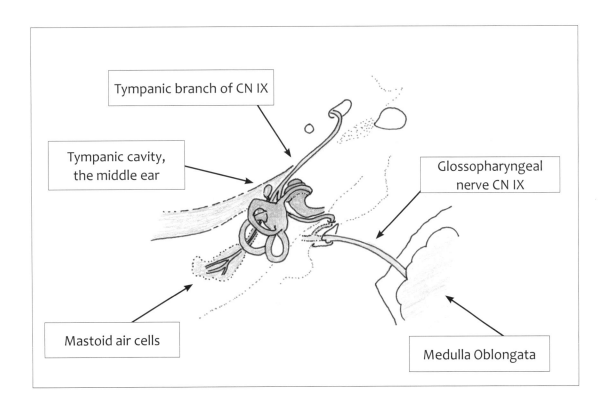

Cranial nerve X

Cranial nerve X shows that:

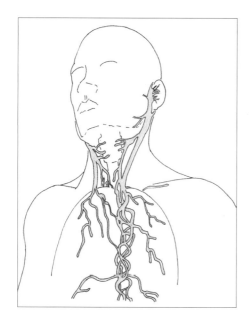

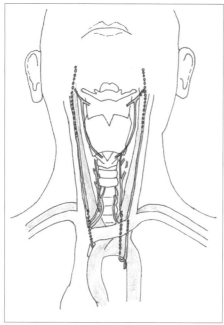

Sound processing through the outer ears is connected to the vagus nerve, cranial nerve X, which in turn connects to most organs in the body and is central to our fight, flight, freeze response.

For sound processing it is especially important to understand that the vagus nerve connections to the larynx are not symmetrical. Sound processing needs to work in balance, but it is an asymmetrical system, hence for most people right-ear dominance is preferable for working with body and brain.

If the sound processing is not working well, it can keep a person in a hyper-alert state. Stimulating the sound processing system can impact on the global sense of safety.

If a person does not feel safe, that will be reflected in their voice quality.

Conversely, habitually clenching the jaw, neck and shoulder area can compromise the vagus nerve and sound processing.

Consider how much a person's voice quality tells you about their emotions.

Cranial nerve XI

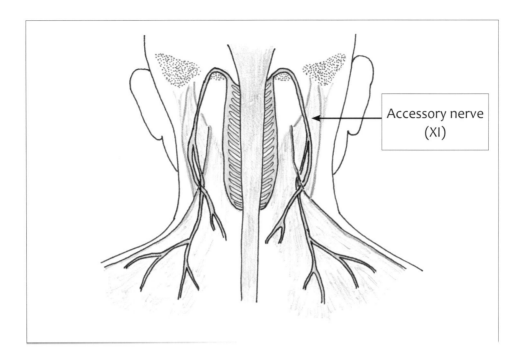

Cranial nerve XI shows that:

The cranial component of this nerve provides motor control to the muscles of the soft palate, larynx and pharynx. So, it is linked to speech.

The spinal component of this nerve provides motor control of the muscles that control the action of shrugging the shoulders, and the action of turning the head.

Turning the head is important in humans, as we do not move our ears. Humans are the only primates who can move their heads separately to their bodies. Developing this movement in infants impacts on the control of their eye muscles, especially when crossing their mid-line. So, this nerve links speech and eye tracking when reading for meaning.

The mid-line in a human is the central line separating left from right sides of the body, brain, eyes, ears and so on. We are born with left and right sides not communicating very well. Ideally as we develop in the first seven or eight years of life left and right sides of motor skills and senses do integrate.

It is possible to see how well a person can mid-line cross by asking them to throw a ball in an arc from one hand to another, without moving their body or head. The person can move their eyes. When there are problems the person might have difficulty not moving their head or bodies; or they might display overflow such as sticking out their tongue, or clenching their jaw, or blinking rapidly. It is also not unusual for people to not be able to throw the ball over their mid-line, instead it falls before the mid-line, or is thrown forwards.

Overview of the cranial nerves

The nerves associated with sound processing have a significant effect on the global functioning of any human. As a child develops from conception to birth, from helpless to crawling and walking upright, the child develops better use of their nervous system. Through growth and engagement with their environment the systems develop and integrate until the human can access all aspects of sound processing and production.

Ideally as a child gains independence they feel secure because their sound processing skills work well, and they feel safe in their environment. When a child's sound processing skills do not develop well, they can continue to go on feeling insecure and hyper-alert. This situation should be resolved for life long good health and cognitive development.

Sound and Porges' long polyvagal theory

Stephen Porges' long polyvagal theory and the relation to sound

The **autonomic nervous system** has two parts which work in balance.

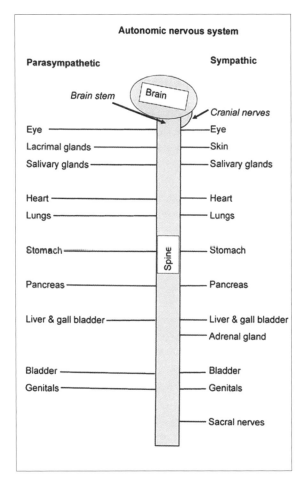

1. The **sympathetic nerves** which automatically prepare the body for fight, flight, freeze.

    - Heart rate increases.
    - Blood pressure increases.
    - Pupil size increases.
    - Blood vessels narrow.
    - Digestive juices decrease.
    - Muscles in the gut tense.

2. The **parasympathetic** nerves which restore the organs to their calm state.

    - Heart rate slows.
    - Blood pressure decreases.
    - Pupil size decreases.
    - Blood vessels dilate.
    - Digestive juices increase.
    - Muscles in the gut relax.

The psychologist Dr Stephen Porges proposed that mammals have evolved the autonomic nervous system which triggers the fight, flight, freeze response as well as social engagement and emotional regulation. It is an unproven theory, but it ties in well with Dr Alfred Tomatis' work on sound processing.

An auditory stimulus takes only 8–10ms to reach the human brain, by comparison a visual stimulus which takes 20–40ms. Sound processing is a human's first alarm system.

Cranial nerve X, the vagus nerve, is involved in both triggering fight, flight, freeze and in calming the body and social engagement. It is a complex nerve that emerges at the ear and is connected to most organs in the body.

The theory provides useful insights to move on modern understanding of human psychology and physiology.

Thoughts and reflections

- Think about when you were very frightened and worried – consider how your body reacted?
- What helped you calm down and feel safe again?
- Think, on a daily basis, does your body change when you get home, and you feel safe and relaxed?

- Think about watching other people in your family and community, how do you know from their body language that they are happy, worried, frightened or distressed?

Strategies for calming the nervous system

Strategies to bring your sensory system to calm

Good mental health is not mysterious, it is simply bringing your body and mind to a coherent, calm state.

As we have evolved, we have developed sophisticated larger brains that can undertake complex tasks, but that part of the brain works quite slowly.

If we are anxious, our old brain takes over and can react very quickly in fight, flight, freeze – we are only intended to stay in this hyper-alert state for minutes. Unfortunately, modern life can keep stimulating a sense of danger and we can get stuck in a hyper-alert state, so we need some strategies to consciously bring our minds and bodies to calm and to think positively.

1. Breathing and heart rate variance

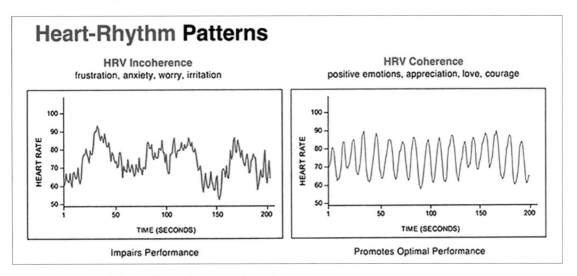

Source: Heartmath https://www.heartmath.org/

When the heart rate is erratic it pumps cortisol to the brain and stops the new brain being able to think calmly. Therefore, a key objective is to bring the heart rate to a coherent state with a smooth, rhythmic pattern.

To make the heart rate coherent the following steps are needed:

(1) Slow rhythmic breathing e.g., breathe out to a count of five, breathe in for a count of five, hold for a count of five and so on.

(2) Breathing through your heart e.g., put your hands on your heart and consciously think about your heart coming to calm.

(3) Think a happy, secure thought (something quite simple and happy e.g., cuddling your mother, or the dog) – learn to focus on that thought as you breath in and out through your heart.

Those three steps should bring your heart rate variance to a coherent state. Practise every day until you just have to think your happy thought and you automatically go into rhythmic breathing, rhythmic heart rate.

If a person habitually focuses on negative thoughts then it is impossible to get the heart rate variance to work coherently. The person must choose to think positively. Starting to think positively can include simple strategies such as counting five good things about their life.

Video links that are useful:

For children and the young at heart: Cosmic Kids Zen Den:

https://www.youtube.com/watch?v=so8QN9an3t8&vl=en-GB

For adults or those who really want to get behind the science: Dr Alan Watkins, Being Brilliant Every Single Day Parts 1 and 2

https://www.youtube.com/watch?v=q06YIWCR2Js

Software that is useful for mastering heart rate variance Heart Math Institute
https://www.heartmath.org/

2.   Nasal Breathing

Learning to breathe through the nose is important, as mouth breathing can deoxygenate the body and hence trigger anxiety.

The way to clear the airways in the head in order to breathe through the nose is to take a deep breath, close your mouth and hold your nose. Move your body from the waist from side to side. Keep holding your breath as long as you can. Then let go and take in a deep breath, breathe normally, blow your nose.

Whilst you are holding your breath, the gasses in the passages in your head are heating up and that causes mucus to melt and clear.

Practicing nasal breathing daily will cause it to eventually become the default mode of breathing. This will improve sleep and global health. It will also keep pathways in the head clear and improve sound processing.

3.   Shaking off trauma

Porges identified that trauma gets held in the body. Over time we hold trauma in and that affects our posture and whole demeanour.

Shaking off trauma is therefore important to reset the sensory system.

Traditionally people shook off trauma by dancing and singing. This is still a very good method, but choose really positive happy songs. Stand up, open your airways fully and really move your whole body to the rhythm.

Other strategies for releasing trauma might include:

- If you are part of a team of workers or a family, it is a very good strategy to have a happy team song. Humans synchronise their body rhythms and get a natural high out of singing and dancing together.
- Note being "in-tune" with others is good for us and it can be as simple as throwing and catching a ball between two people or playing games where you name five things each that you can hear, see and touch.
- Modern lifestyles mean that many humans have bad postural habits that cause them to keep going into positions that hold trauma and block breathing. Design spaces so that people habitually sit or stand in good postures.

Posture and open airways

Humans function best with an upright posture and with open airways. Experience with clients is that they often cannot stop themselves going back into postures that trigger anxiety, so they need to retrain their bodies with strategies such as:

- Only read computers, books and other material when they are raised, so they can easily be read whilst keeping the head reasonably upright.
- When moving about, practise keeping the head upright and from time to time look at videos of their own movements.
- Do exercises that promote upright posture: (a) Patsy Rodenburg has several useful videos online to train actors, but they are equally useful for people working with anxiety: https://vimeo.com/51564143 (b) Jeanette Nelson, Head of Voice, National Theatre: https://www.youtube.com/watch?v=7_MvlGKwLho&list=RDwKqPjCR69yM&index=7

Stretching the long polyvagal nerve by lying prone.

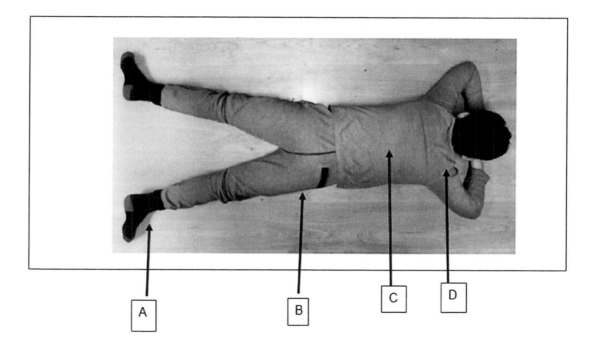

Note this is a great position to adopt in order to calm a person as it stretches the long polyvagal nerve and opens the airways. People can lie in this position for up to ten minutes before sleeping or when they cannot stop feeling very anxious and combined with rhythmic breathing it brings people back to a calm and coherent state.

A. By pressing gently on the heels, the legs are turned gently in relation to the hips. That puts the leg in the right position with the hips and stops the legs turning inwards and pressing down on the feet and feet arches.

B. When the hips are in the right position with the legs they also fall into the correct position with the hips.

C. The spine can then establish a good position.

D. Also, the shoulders are pushed back.

4. Sound and trauma

Trauma can get badly trapped in sound processing. It is often very obvious, as we will see in some of the case studies on pages 74–101. Sound therapy is therefore a very useful tool to shake off trauma and to work with other therapies to bring a person to calm.

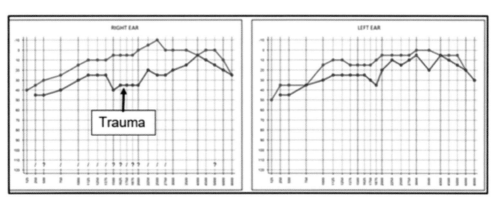

Sound processing profile of a traumatised person

Key: Blue curve = sound processing through air conduction of sound;
Red curve = sound conduction through bone conduction of sound;
Red / and ? = points where the direction of sound is confused.
X axis = Hertz from 125Hz to 8,000Hz; Y axis = Decibels (-10Db to 120Db)

When a person is traumatized, they close down their sound processing to protect themselves and to stop themselves feeling the pain. That helps humans to physically survive, but emotionally it leaves scars and that can be seen when you screen a person for sound processing.

Good sound processing improves global wellbeing by agitating the vestibular system in the inner ear that helps shake off anxiety.

In the case studies in the following chapter, it will be seen that sound therapy shakes off held trauma, which can be clearly seen in the way the sound processing functions.

Once the sound processing works properly the person feels more joyous in themselves.

5. Relaxing the jaw area

Many people habitually clench their jaw, for a variety of reasons. This can be a problem because it puts pressure on the nerves around the neck, jaw and vestibular area (inner ear) and can cause problems with tinnitus, migraines, and generally working coherently with all senses.

It is, therefore, a useful strategy to learn to relax the jaw to stop the side effects.

To relax the jaw, do the following:

(a)   Just shake your head with a relaxed jaw and feel the jaw being relaxed. Some people need practise this – keep trying, it is worth it.

(b)   Lie in the Alexander Technique "constructive rest" position (https:// www.alexandertechnique.com/constructiverest/) with jaw relaxed. You may need help to do this, so ask a friend to watch you or video yourself whilst you lie there so you can see if you tighten up your jaw again very quickly.

Adaptation of Alexander Technique constructive rest position, the jaw is relaxed.

(c)   Ask your friends to remind you to relax your jaw.

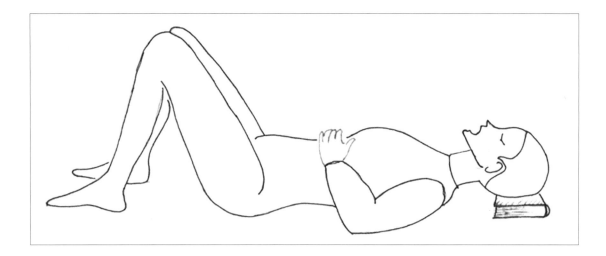

3

How sound processing develops from conception

Post-birth development of sound processing

The impact of modern lifestyles

How sound processing develops from conception

Sound processing is our first myelinated sense. The inner ear is the only sense organ to develop fully before birth. After birth, sound processing skills go on developing, and stimulation from sound triggers a lot of development in other areas such as motor skills and vision.

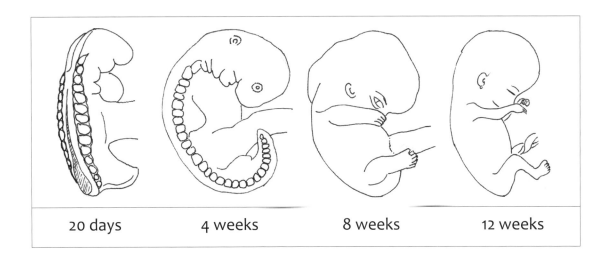

| 20 days | 4 weeks | 8 weeks | 12 weeks |

Above is the standard view of the developing human in the womb from twenty days to twelve weeks of life.

For sound processing it is important to know what is happening in these very first days to understand how the whole body is involved in making sense of sound and producing sound in speech.

Like all animals, from conception humans divide cells and as those cells divide and multiple they create the foundations for all organs to develop according to the pattern determined by our genetic code. The division of the cells in a specific pattern means that there are connections between a diverse range of organs.

Consequently, sound processing is connected to all parts of the body, and as the body develops so does sound processing. Conversely, problems with development will impact on development of sound processing.

Key stages of foetal development

Note that the womb is a noisy place: the mother's heartbeat, digestive system and blood flow are all creating sounds which surround the developing foetus. The foetus is surrounded by fluid, so any sound processing consists of vibrations coming through the fluid, which filters the sounds that the foetus perceives.

- By the end of the fourth week, the face and eyes begin to develop, and the heart begins to beat. The baby will be slightly smaller than a grain of rice, but it will be creating a rhythmic heartbeat. Rhythm is an important part of sound processing.
- At about five weeks after conception the cochlea, middle ear and outer ear all start forming, these structures take many more weeks to mature and send signals to the brain.
- Also, at about this time organs such as the brain, sensory organs, and the digestive tract begin to take shape. The cartilage in the embryo begins to be replaced by bone. After about six weeks, the baby's heartbeat can be detected with an ultrasound.
- By seven to eight weeks the foetus begins to move.
- By eight weeks, the foetus has developed the sense of touch. Through touch the foetus will feel the vibrations of sound.
- By the tenth week the vocal cords are forming and linked to the pharynx and trachea.
- By week 14 the limbs, as well as the hands, feet, fingers and toes, become well developed. The fingernails and toenails begin to form. The external ears and teeth begin their development as well.
- At 14 to 15 weeks all the movements the foetus will make have emerged.
- By 15 weeks the foetus responds to flavours of the amniotic fluid.
- By 19 weeks the nervous system develops.
- By 20 weeks the vestibular labyrinth (also known as the semi-circular canals) has made its way to the neural tube. The semi-circular canals are responsible for sensing angular head motion in three-dimensional space and for providing neural inputs to the central nervous system essential for agile mobility, stable vision, and autonomic control of the cardiovascular and other gravity-sensitive systems. As this develops it controls the motor system.

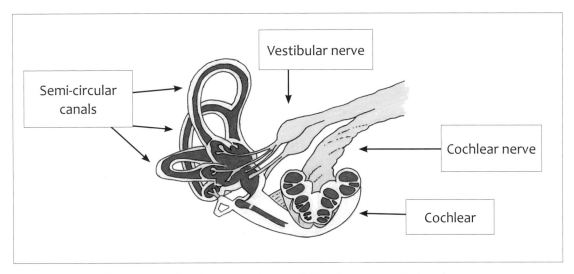

By 20 weeks the structure of the inner ear is in place.

- By the end of week 20, all major microscopic features of the tachea are visible, but it is short and narrow while the larynx is relatively long. This relationship remains until after birth when the trachea outgrows the larynx to reach its final form.
- At about the same time, the cochlear reaches out to the rest of the brain to record sounds.
- From 22 to 24 weeks the foetus responds to sound initially only in low frequencies 250Hz to 500Hz.
- From 28 to 30 weeks the foetus requires auditory experience with voice and language, music and meaningful environmental sounds to develop fully. The foetus is starting to learn the patterns of language around them. The eyelids become parted, and the eyes can be opened. The baby will respond to external stimuli such as sounds by increasing their pulse or moving.
- By week 29 hearing is fully developed. The foetus will react to sound, pain and light and often changes position.
- By week 34 the foetus can see and will begin to kick more. Most of the internal organs and systems are fully developed, but the lungs still need time to mature.
- By week 40 the lungs become mature in preparation for birth. Reflexes become more coordinated, allowing the baby to respond to sounds, blink, grasp, and turn their head. The baby may move less during the last few weeks and will move into a position for birth.

Preterm infants should not be exposed to over 60 decibels. The foetus has sensitive sound processing, and it can be damaged if subject to high volumes of noise. The advice is not to put sound devices like speakers or headphones at high volumes near the womb or a premature baby.

Post-birth development of sound processing

Within six weeks of birth the infant has tuned its ear to its mother tongue and blocked out sounds that are not needed to communicate with those immediately around them.

Each language uses a distinctive range of sound in hertz and pronunciation.

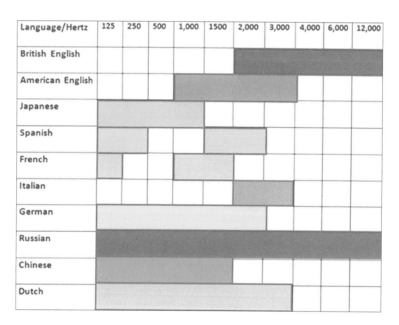

Language/Hertz	125	250	500	1,000	1500	2,000	3,000	4,000	6,000	12,000
British English										
American English										
Japanese										
Spanish										
French										
Italian										
German										
Russian										
Chinese										
Dutch										

The ear goes on developing after birth in the way it integrates with the nervous system and the brain until at least the second year of life.

As the child's postural control develops so does the ability to make sense of sounds. Adult postural control is not in place until seven years of age, assuming the child develops well.

At around six years of age a child naturally moves from left to right ear dominant. This increases the speed at which young children can process sounds.

If a child has had problems with sound processing such as trauma or inner ear infection, this shift in ear dominance may not happen and the person can experience a delay in sound processing unless there is a sound therapy intervention.

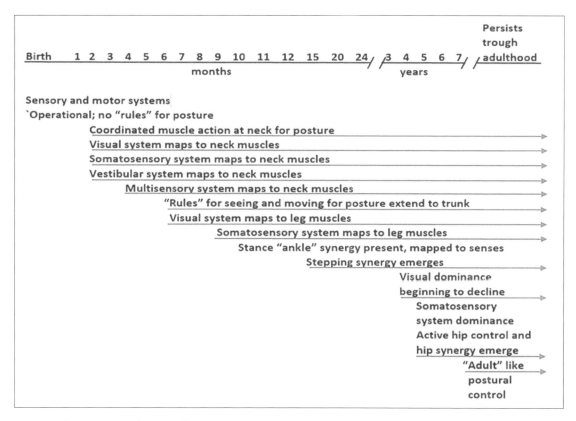

Source: Shumway-Cook & Woollacott, Motor Control, 2017

Postural control development coincides with the development of speech. How children speak is a good indication of how they process sounds. The table below provides an indication of the typical ages by which children master certain sounds.

- Around 3 years: b, p, m, n, h, d, k, g, ng (sing), t, w, f, y
- Around 4-5 years: f, sh, zh, ch, j, s, and cluster sounds tw, kw, gl, bl
- Around 6 years l, r, v, ng, and cluster sounds pl, kl, kr, fl, tr, st, dr, br, fr, gr, sn, sk, sw, sp, str, spl
- Around 7-8 years: th, z, and cluster sounds sm, sl, thr, skw, spr, skr

Phonological development: A normative study of British English-speaking children, Dodds et al (2003)

Development of the voice box during childhood

Before birth the trachea is short and narrow while the larynx is relatively long. This relationship remains until after birth when the trachea outgrows the larynx to reach its final form.

At about three months of age in the human, the larynx descends to a position in the pharynx opening the airway to the nose, allowing breathing through the mouth instead of just the nose, and improving air pressure during crying.

During infancy, the vocal structure begins to develop into a miniature version of the adult's. While a newborn's vocal tract has evolved for survival (burbling, screaming and crying), the child's and adult's is set up for speaking and running.

The infant's larynx grows and descends lower down the trachea and the lungs grow comparatively larger to the digestive system. This gives them much more range and flexibility in the sounds they are able to make, though the adult setup won't be complete until the age of eight or nine.

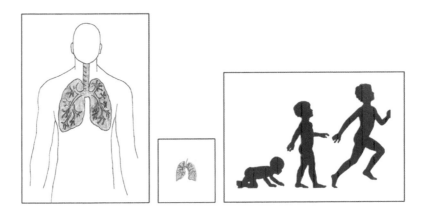

The infant has to deal each day with physiological changes and at the same time learn to control and manipulate an ever-changing body. That process needs to be monitored, encouraged and supported to ensure that all children achieve complete physical mastery.

This area of physiology, of course makes another big change in adolescence when the pitch of the voice drops, particularly for boys.

For some people their larynx does not drop fully, and this leaves them feeling hyper-alert which can manifest as shyness or, in extremis, mutism. For such people it is worth undertaking primitive reflex exercises which can help the larynx drop lower in the trachea. This dropping of the larynx quickly makes the person feel considerably more grounded and confident. Primitive reflex exercises are outlined on pages 110 onwards.

Eustachian tube

The Eustachian tube in infancy differs anatomically and physiologically from that of the adolescent. In infancy, the Eustachian tube is shorter (18mm) and has a more acute angle (10°) compared with the length (36mm) and angle (45°) during adolescence and adulthood.

This means that infants have a high incidence of inner ear infections. As posture develops and people spend more time in activities that require an upright posture then the ear should drain better through the eustachian tube.

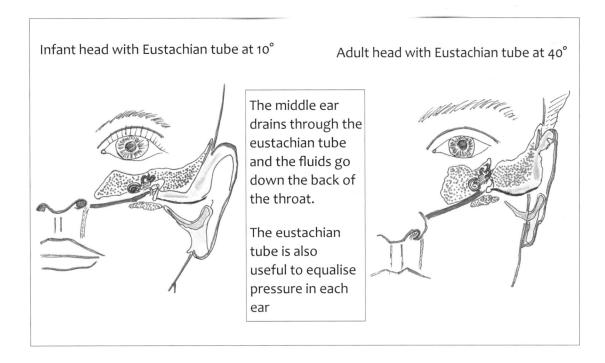

Infant head with Eustachian tube at 10°

Adult head with Eustachian tube at 40°

The middle ear drains through the eustachian tube and the fluids go down the back of the throat.

The eustachian tube is also useful to equalise pressure in each ear

Inner ear infection can cause problems with temporary deafness and can leave the middle ear muscles weakened.

Also, sedentary modern lifestyles can cause the Eustachian tube not to function properly as people are often not upright for extended periods.

The impact of modern lifestyles

In industrialised societies people are eating hyper-processed foods from birth and this is impacting on the development of teeth and bones. Over the last 300 years human faces have got flatter and lower jaws have got smaller. This has narrowed the airways and restricted space for teeth in the mouth. This process has accelerated in recent years.

The dental profession and doctors working with obesity are extremely concerned about the impact of processed foods on modern health and fitness.

The first commercial baby food was a vegetable soup with a beef broth base. Other common baby foods in the 1940s included liver, veal and strained single-ingredient vegetables and fruits. By the 1950s, however, baby food companies increased their focus on taste, adding sugar and artificial flavours, as well as food that was a more consistent, smooth purée. The US trend for commercial baby food spread rapidly across the developed world. Just stand in your local supermarket and observe what we are feeding infants. It does not look good!

The airways in the head need to work and drain properly in order to maintain the functioning of the sound processing. Flatter faces and narrower airways are compromising that process and exacerbating the incidence of inner ear infection.

Further, humans are far more sedentary than in the past. A hunter-gatherer would typically walk 9.5kms a day, day in day out. A modern Londoner on average walks 1.2km a day (2017–18). We have comfortable homes, and many people lie down for extended periods on sofas and on their beds with computer devices. Many people also hunch over for hours at home and at work in positions that restrict good functioning of the whole body.

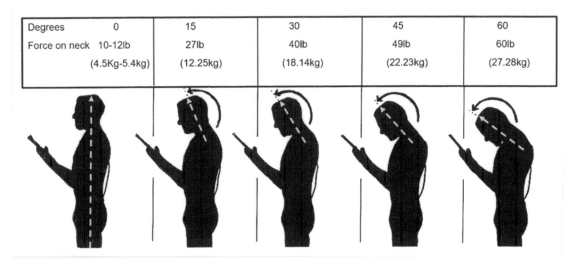

Degrees	0	15	30	45	60
Force on neck	10-12lb (4.5Kg-5.4kg)	27lb (12.25kg)	40lb (18.14kg)	49lb (22.23kg)	60lb (27.28kg)

A distorted posture not only causes pain when it pressurises nerves, it also restricts good sound processing.

Humans have not evolved to operate in modern environments. To maximise sound processing and overall body health it is strongly recommended that people create environments in their homes and at work that maximise upright posture, good breathing and movement.

Plan with your family at home, and your colleagues at work, spaces that maximise light and air. Furniture that gives the opportunity to work upright sitting or standing. Exercises that break extended periods on a screen or in any fixed position such as:

- Stretching limbs.
- Breathing nasally and rhythmically.
- Eye exercises.
- Have meetings walking.

- Find opportunities to play games and sing songs to bring the team/family into tune with each other to solve problems.
- Think about the acoustics of your environment, consider simple strategies that will reduce reverberations and background noise.

Infants and children's sound processing and speech skills need to be supported with a lot of activities to build skills in rhythm, speech and singing.

It is never too late to start even if you are an adult and need some help with Tomatis technology.

If a family does not have a tradition of reciting rhymes and singing songs to infants and children, it takes a bit of thought to gather resources together. Below is a list of possible activities that you can undertake. In the appendix are a list of rhymes, poems and songs that we think that every child should know by eight years of age.

If you are raising a child to be bilingual make sure that you have resources in both languages and both culture's rhythms.

If you want your child to learn a language but do not feel confident, then use recordings.

- Sing along to songs together from high quality recordings.
- Have a family "happy" song for the year and sing and dance to it in the kitchen every day.
- Infants benefit from traditional rhymes and songs that are slow. The speech is called "Motherese". It slowly emphasises the language sounds. Rhymes like "Patter cake, patter cake, baker's man" are normally recited slowly.
- Read books aloud with the child that have a clear rhythmic pattern. In English such books might be: *We're Going on a Bear Hunt*, *The Gruffalo*, *A Squash and a Squeeze*, *Room on the Broom*, *Peepo*, *Each Peach Pear Plum* and so on. The books need to be read over and over until every member of the family knows them off by heart.
- Babies benefit from being walked around by family members whilst they recite nursery rhymes, such as "Rock-a-bye Baby".

- When you walk along to the shops and the park use songs and rhymes to keep the child going.
- Play hand-clapping games with rhymes.
- Use a metronome running at 54bpm to help establish rhythmic movements. 54bpm is a relatively slow beat which gives the child time to maintain their current skills and learn a new skill.
- By the time a child is five or six years old they are likely to take an interest in children's musical theatre. This is another opportunity to repeatedly watch a film until the child knows every word of every song.
- Join groups that encourage musical activities. Boogie Mites, for example, run well-organised and researched musical activities https://www.boogiemites.co.uk/
- Look up traditional singing and movement songs and learn them and act them out until they are family favourites. This is one such YouTube channel: https://www.youtube.com/@AndSoToBedTV/videos

4

Dr Alfred Tomatis

Sound therapy in practice

Case studies pre-six-years-old

Case studies of older children and adults

Sound processing and therapy in practice

Dr Alfred Tomatis (1920–2001)

Modern sound therapy began with Dr Alfred Tomatis. He was a French ear nose and throat doctor who worked with high performing musicians and industrial workers in the time whilst he developed his understanding of how living humans process sound.

In 1957, he submitted the "Tomatis Laws" to the Academy of Sciences in Paris. These laws established that:

- The voice only contains what the ear can hear.
- If the listening is modified, the voice is instantly and unconsciously modified too.
- It is possible to transform the voice permanently through sound stimulation maintained for some time (law of remanence).

All modern forms of sound therapy are developments from Tomatis' work.

Tomatis further observed that the ear plays an important role in posture, balance and muscle tone.

He developed the hypothesis of auditory laterality and the existence of a dominant ear.

Further, he was one of the first specialists to discover and point out that the foetus hears from the eighteenth week of pregnancy and that the ear plays a major role in cognitive development. He then established that intrauterine listening is critical to emotional development.

A key element of Tomatis' work is that the living human processes sound through:

(a) bone conduction – i.e., their whole body

(b) through air conduction – i.e., air coming through their auditory canal.

That these two systems must work together coherently in order for a person to make good sense of the sound around them.

On pages 68 onwards we will look at case studies and consider what that means and how sound therapy can change a person's cognitive processing.

Sound therapy in practice

What is sound therapy and how does it work?

Sound therapy comes in various forms, but the basic concept is that it is using specialised technology to agitate the tiny muscles in the middle ear, which in turn agitates the inner ear and change the way the brain perceives sound.

Let's take that all apart...

Generally sound therapy requires a specialised headset and specialised music.

Bone conduction device in the headset. This transmits the music through the cranium to the ear.

Therefore, throughout listening the person keeps the top of the headphones in contact with their head.

Earphones transmit the music to the person through the ear canal i.e., this is air conduction of sound.

The design of the headset means that sound is coming to the ear through both bone and air conduction of sound.

- Bone conduction works much faster than air conduction of sound. So, the bone conduction of sound agitates the middle ear first. The ear naturally dampens down vibrations once they have been received.
- Air conduction of sound then arrives and agitates the middle ear. Again once the message has been received the ear naturally dampens down vibrations.

Hence, the headsets are designed to agitate both air and bone conduction of sound and to maximise movement of the ear muscles and subsequent processing through the inner ear to the brain.

The specialised music

For some forms of Tomatis sound therapy the music is all preloaded and built into the headsets. For intensive rounds of sound therapy with a consultant it is possible to see more of how the music works.

All the music is in two bands and the music erratically moves from one band to another. The music is the same, but one band of music has had the higher sounds removed and the other band has had the lower sounds removed. This is because it needs to alert the brain to respond to sound. If it did not change or was predictable, the ear and the brain would ignore it and the ear muscles would not move as much.

The vast majority of the music used is either by Mozart, or Gregorian chant. Tomatis identified that this music had characteristics that maximised the movement of the ear and brain without emotionally dysregulating people.

There are well-designed standard programmes, and consultants can design their own programmes, but they work within carefully defined parameters.

Whilst the person listens to the sound therapy, their ear is responding to the music in the following order:

(a) Bone conduction of sound;

(b) Air conduction of sound;

Band of music changes

(c) Bone conduction of sound;

(d) Air conduction of sound;

Band of music changes

And so on for up 80 minutes a day for 14 days.

It is not necessary to listen to the music, it is possible to get on and do other things, even sleep.

Alternative devices

It is not always possible or convenient to wear headphones.

(a)   Babies and infants

Infants that do not go to full-term or who have difficult births or who have genetic issues, such as Down's Syndrome may have problems with their sound processing from the start. It is not possible for them to use headphones as their skull is not yet fully formed.

The fontanelle in the human skull is the soft spot on the child's skull. The bones in the skull are not usually closed until the child is 18 months old.

However, it is possible to stimulate sound processing using a bone conduction device and specially adapted music. This is useful for stimulating global development in the infant.

(b)   Hyper-alert and traumatised people

Some people are so traumatised that they cannot bear sound therapy through a headset. In such situations just putting sound therapy through the base of the spine can be a useful strategy to release held trauma.

This is useful when people are trapped in a loop of needing help, but by reflex rejecting all help.

Forbrain

Forbrain is a device that works with just bone conduction of sound but is stimulated by the human voice.

In order for the device to work, the person has to talk into it. It is a much less intrusive device than headphones, however, some people really cannot bear to hear themselves speak.

It is, though, possible to use it whilst you work, if your employment requires you to speak and can have a good impact on sound processing skills at the same time. It can easily be incorporated into a daily routine.

The author used the device to boost alertness when driving. It is a useful device to fine-tune global skills, because like all sound therapy it triggers a wide range of senses and motor skills.

A Forbrain device works well with speech therapy and foreign language learning. It is also a useful device for singing teachers.

Case studies – pre-six-years-old

It is quite hard to formally assess a child of six years and under for sound processing skills. They are not yet developed enough to get accurate results. However, it is possible to get a fair estimate just by listening to their speech.

Tomatis' basic rule that: "The voice only contains what the ear can hear" holds true.

Consequently, the best way to assess a very young child, or an older person who has issues that make a formal assessment difficult, is to observe them speaking and playing with sounds.

- It is recommended that you video what you see. It is very easy to forget where a person started from if you do not keep a record.
- It is also useful to keep photographs of the person standing upright from the side and the front. Then it is possible to observe any changes to postural control which happen as a result of sound therapy.
- If the client can draw, then it is also useful to ask them to draw before and after an intervention. Then it is possible to capture how sound impacts on global development. This can be a powerful piece of evidence of the impact of sound therapy on global development.

Before 3 months' work on sound and motor skills   **After 3 months' work on sound and motor skills**

The image above very powerfully shows the impact of sound therapy with other motor skills therapies on a youngster's development. At the start the child is seeing left and right sides of their mid-line in different colours and the image is scribbled – i.e., the child struggles with visual and motor skills control. After sound therapy the child has jumped in basic global development.

Think about children or adults you know. Consider how access to sound therapy could support them to fine-tune their motor skills and senses.

Case studies of older children and adults

Formal assessment

Formal assessment for sound processing skills is possible from six years onwards.

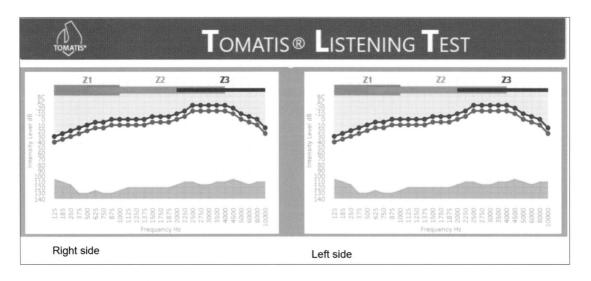

Above is an idealised screenshot of a sound processing test.

The blue curve marks the client's perception of sound on air conduction across the sound range from 125Hz to 10,000Hz. Along the Y axis are marked the decibels.

This reading is taken by asking a person to wear headphones and indicate as soon as they can hear anything, and on which side.

This is the best sound processing curve that is possible for a human. It is the ideal and is the target that is worked towards when undertaking sound therapy.

The red curve marks the client's perception of sound on bone conduction across the sound range from 125Hz to 10,000Hz.

This reading is taken by placing a device on the bone behind the person's ear, but not touching the pinna (the external ear). The person is asked to indicate as soon as they can hear anything and on which side.

This is an ideal curve for processing sound through bone conduction. The curve lies below the air conduction and runs along parallel with a gap of 10 decibels.

Balance: The therapist and the client should step back and look at the curves overall and consider whether there is balance between left and right sides.

Just from these curves the client would be expected to have upright posture, very clear well-articulated speech, and no overflow around the jaw area.

Further tests: The client will be tested for their ability to pitch differentiate – i.e., can the client accurately identify whether one sound is higher or lower than another sound at various points along the sound range being tested?

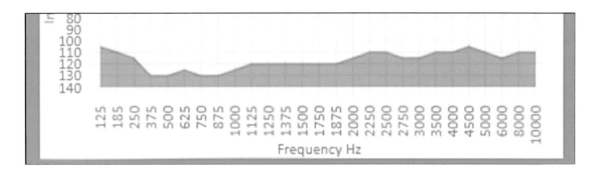

This is a really important skill and impacts on a person's ability to understand another person's speech in context, particularly whether speech is friendly or aggressive.

Language can change meaning if the intonation is misinterpreted. Think about the simple sentences:

- Would you like to come to lunch then?
- What is that in your hand?
- This is your car.

Some people cannot tell if the message is friendly, neutral or aggressive because they struggle to differentiate between pitch of sounds.

- Consider how hard it is for a police officer trying to communicate with a person when the person's sound processing is disrupted, and the person cannot tell if any speech is friendly or aggressive.

- Think about how often sensitive children feel they are being shouted at when the teacher or parent is speaking in a normal tone of voice. Think whether the problem could lie in basic sound processing.

Laterality can also be tested – i.e., whether a person is left or right ear dominant and how easily they can follow sounds when they move. Again, it is important to ensure that the person does not have a microsecond delay on their sound processing and to ensure that the person can follow a moving speaker. Poor laterality can make functioning in a classroom very difficult as the teacher moves round the class and the delay on processing means that it takes time for the student to respond if they can at all. They will know that the teacher is talking, but think that they are not concentrating because they cannot make sense of the speech.

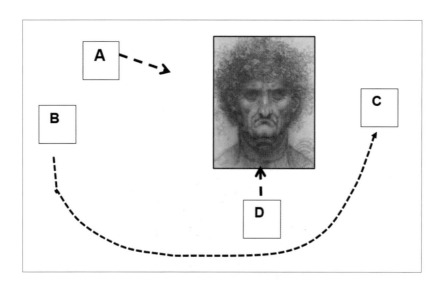

A person is at all times calculating where sounds are coming from and following sounds as they move relative to their two ears. So, the person in the diagram person knows that person A is behind and D is in front, just from sound. They should be able to follow a person when they move from point B to point C, making adjustments as the sound moves.

That is a lot of processing to be doing in microseconds and if it does not work well that can build in microsecond delays that seem like nothing, but in fact make sound very difficult to understand. The person knows that there is a sound; but finds it difficult to make sense of it. They might cover their ears to protect themselves or go away from loud and irritating sounds.

It is not common to see curves like the one at the start of this section, but it is useful to know what our sound processing target is so that we can understand less perfect sound processing curves and how they might impact on a person.

In the following pages we will look at a variety of case studies so that it is possible to understand how sound processing can be compromised and how it can be recovered.

Case studies

When you look at sound processing curves you must be aware that the body really does hold the score and that can easily be seen in the constrained sound processing curves.

It is also possible to move most sound processing curves towards the ideal and give a person far better one, which will impact on many aspects of their lives.

Person A

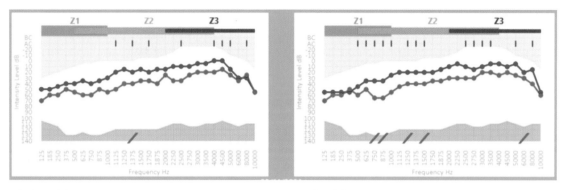

Right side   Left side

Client: Middle-aged female

What can be seen?

The blue marks (I) along the top of the screenshots show the points at which the person struggles with pitch differentiation i.e., they are not sure if one sound is higher or lower than another sound. That impacts on the person's ability to understand speech or written text in context.

The red marks along the bottom of the screenshots show the points where the person struggles to the identify direction of sound on bone conduction. This is not a huge problem, but it is slightly disrupting messages going from ear to brain.

On both sides, the air conduction of sound is suppressed up to 25 decibels below the location of the ideal curve. This is not surprising in a middle-aged person. Humans naturally close down their sound processing as they are worn down by life. The good news is that Tomatis sound therapy can help move these curves up closer to the ideal.

The air and bone conduction of sound do not work together coherently. There are points where the two curves clash and there are points where there are big gaps of more than 10 decibels between the two curves. Again, that disrupts the message going from ear to brain.

The two sides of the sound processing are sufficiently different that they do not work together coherently. Further, another sub-test has indicated that the person is struggling to follow sound and is left-ear dominant, so there is a microsecond delay on their sound processing.

Lots of small problems with sound processing can make it hard work to follow speech in a meeting or a social occasion. It is exhausting and the person develops a preference for quiet environments and smaller gatherings. Their world gets smaller.

When sound closes down, that also impacts on vision and sense of space. Consequently, opening up sound processing opens up a person's global senses and sense of confidence. The person is less worn down by life. Further, better access to good sound processing gives a person a better perception of music and social engagement which makes them feel more joyous.

Visualise this person...

Middle-aged, female maybe has two children, a job and a husband. Perhaps also elderly relatives who need taking care of. They have many demands on their life.

Think about how that is reflected in their physiology. What does this person look like if you met them in a café?

Women at this stage of life tend to be in lower paying work, with less job security. Low status and economic insecurity can also wear down a person's sound processing.

Consider practical steps this person could undertake to support themselves to get better sound processing skills and to maintain themselves better.

- Build walking into their routine, rather than driving.
- Put together a favourite music list that they can sing along and dance to whilst cooking and cleaning.
- Use wearable Tomatis sound therapy technology as part of a daily routine. Over time the sound curves will rise and as she ages the curves will be maintained.

N.B. Men can look just as worn down... a common issue is that they have to keep jobs that they do not like in order to pay the bills. The weight of the responsibility, the sense that there is no option, and the strain of endearing themselves to difficult employers is visible on their sound curves.

Person B Male Teacher in 50s

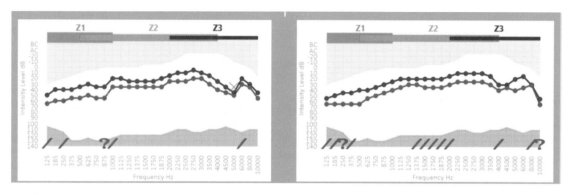

Right side   Left side

Client: Male Teacher in their 50s in a high-achieving school

What can be seen?

The air (blue) and bone (red) conduction of sound run along on both sides relatively coherently for most of the reading. A bit suppressed throughout by about 20 decibels, which reflects the normal wear and tear of life. Then something significant has affected the person on both sides at about the 4000Hz point that has caused them to significantly close down their sound processing. Above that point sound processing on both sides is clashing and scrambling.

No problems were noted with pitch differentiation or directionality.

The sound curves tend to reflect a person's lifespan from birth to present. Birth being at the lowest point in the sound range and present day being at the highest point in the sound range.

Four years prior to this reading the senior management at this person's school had changed. Like many senior teachers, the new team were not trained in Human Resources management, and were not skilled in managing staff, or following up complaints in a professional balanced manner. The aggressive manner of the new management team caused one member of staff to commit suicide and this person to take long-term sick leave and eventually win a case for constructive dismissal.

"The UK has more than twice the proportion of teachers aged under 30 than other developed countries, and pay is below the international average at all comparable levels of education."

Independent, September 2019 reporting on OECD data.

The person eventually removed themselves from the toxic environment and undertook sound therapy. The sound curves after one round of therapy moved so that the person was able to shake off the trauma and move on to another role.

Visualise this person...

A fit, professional, well-respected man who has worked at the forefront of his profession for decades. Whose face does not fit when the new young management come in. He is respected both inside and outside the school and has a solid reputation nationally for his work in extracurricular activities.

Marie-France Hirigoyen documented gaslighting in the workplace well in her book *Stealing the Soul* (2000). People define themselves by their work and their work relationships. Teaching is a particularly complex profession from that perspective. Teachers work alone for much of the day and catch quick conversations with colleagues during breaks. They can be easily isolated. They are vulnerable to false accusations by pupils. Conversely, pupils are young, their perception of reality and consequences of their actions is not fully formed.

Sound is our first survival mechanism; it closes down when a person feels threatened. If sound is closed down for an extended period then it can get stuck. That impacts on all aspects of processing, via the vestibular system. It is not possible to do a job that requires cognitive skills at the highest level if the person feels under attack. The person needs to be in a safe space to move on from such a trauma.

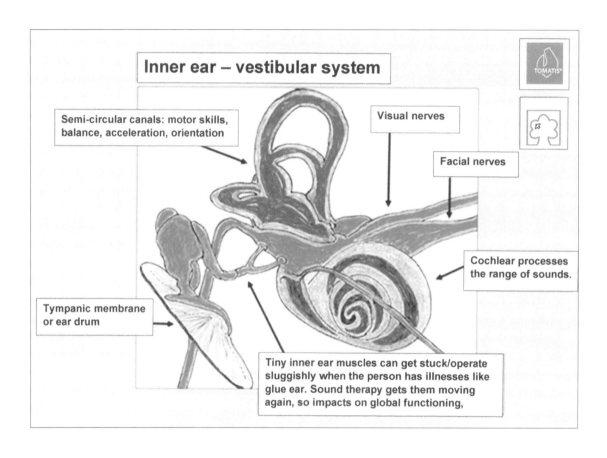

Inner ear – vestibular system

Semi-circular canals: motor skills, balance, acceleration, orientation

Visual nerves

Facial nerves

Cochlear processes the range of sounds.

Tympanic membrane or ear drum

Tiny inner ear muscles can get stuck/operate sluggishly when the person has illnesses like glue ear. Sound therapy gets them moving again, so impacts on global functioning,

Person C

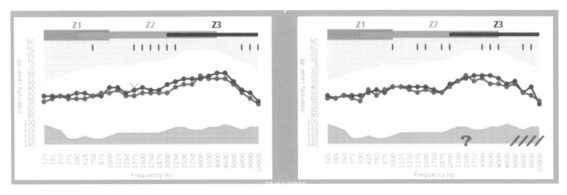

Right side   Left side

Client: Middle-aged female, domestic abuse victim

What can be seen?

The blue marks along the top of the screenshots show the points at which the person struggles with pitch differentiation – i.e., they are not sure if one sound is higher or lower than another sound. That impacts on the person's ability to understand speech or written text in context.

The red marks along the bottom of the screenshots show the points where the person struggles to identify direction of sound on bone conduction.

On both sides the air conduction of sound is suppressed by up to 45 decibels below the location of the ideal curve. This is more than just the wear and tear of a normal life. It is a person closing down their sound processing in order to survive a very hostile environment for a very long period. It is possible to move the curves up, but not until the person feels in a safe place. That is that they are not just in a safe space, but that they feel safe and are open to opening up their sound processing.

The air (blue curve) and the bone (red curve) conduction of sound clash across the whole sound range. I would expect that to be reflected in the person's posture, habitually curling in and tightening of muscles around the head and neck. To get the sound curves to move it will also be helpful to get the person to open up their posture and strengthen their postural control.

The curves are relatively flat, and the person was emotionally flat. Their sound is severely suppressed, and they are not feeling the joys of life, they are hyper-alert. They do not feel able to drop their guard.

Doing sound therapy lifts the curves so that they separate and work together more coherently. The sound therapy shakes off the trauma and opens a more joyous life to the person.

Visualise this person....

Empowering women to live without violence and fear.

Refuge is the largest domestic abuse organisation in the UK. On any given day our services support thousands of women and their children, helping them to overcome the physical, emotional, financial and logistical impacts of abuse and rebuild their lives — free from fear.

https://refuge.org.uk/

They might have two children who are economically dependent. They are frightened of their partner and have been intimidated physically and/or emotionally for an extended period. They might also be holding down a job, where they also attract bullying behaviour. They might be worried for their children's safety and that might worry them more than their own safety. They might be trying to keep up appearances and not want other people to know the situation that they are in; they feel shame. They might have parents or friends who do not understand. They feel completely isolated.

All of these factors drive down a person's sound processing curves. The person is habitually in fight, flight, freeze. They have got stuck in hyper-vigilance.

In order to move on:

- They need to be in a physically safe space.
- They need to believe that they are really safe so that they are safe enough to consciously or unconsciously not block every approach to help.

- Sound therapy can gently help to reduce a state of hyper-alertness, but other therapies such as breathing and managing heart rate variance may also be necessary. Neurofeedback and red-light therapy are producing interesting results with severely traumatised people.
- They need a supportive community and some hobbies or activities that give more meaning to their life.
- It is highly likely their children will also need help to open up their sound processing when they feel safe.

Person D

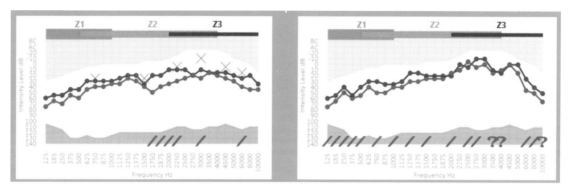

Right side   Left side

Client: Teenager in a pupil referral unit

What can be seen?

This person has not been tested for pitch differentiation skills or for ear dominance. These tests are more demanding and not all clients can access them.

There are significant differences between the two sides of the sound processing. The sound processing curves are high and not far from the ideal, but they look very chaotic.

On the left side of the sound processing curves for air (blue curve) and for bone (red curve) conduction of sound are clashing across the sound range from 125Hz to 10,000Hz. That is scrambling messages going from ear to brain. Children who have been excluded from school have struggled in education for years and this wears them down emotionally, this may account for some of the confusion that can be seen.

Also it can be seen, on the left side, that there are many red dashes at the bottom of the screen. This shows that understanding of direction of sound on bone conduction is confused across the sound range.

The youngster has separately been identified as having significant problems with crossing their mid-line. This causes them to tighten the area around their jaw and neck every time they work across their mid-line. This may impact on the confusion around bone conduction of sound.

On the right side of the sound processing there are blue crosses which indicate that there is confusion about direction of sound on air conduction of sound. This is a common sign that the person has had severe inner ear infection.

Also, on the right side there are some clashes between air (blue) and bone (red) curves of sound.

On both sides there are odd dips in the sound curves which may emotionally destabilise the person.

The objective for this young person is to undertake therapy to remove all the confusion on both air and bone conduction of sound and to raise the sound processing curves so that the two curves do not clash and do not have any dips, but are coherent arcs.

It is possible to move the sound curves, but it can be hard to sustain if the person does not also sort out their problems with mid-line crossing and posture. Also, if the person does not feel safe in the home or school environment.

Visualise this person....

There they are at the bus stop eating chips and messing about with their friends. Sit nearby and watch.

The British film *Kes* (1969) directed by Ken Loach is a good depiction of that sort of youngster. More recently the documentary *H is for Harry* follows a youngster struggling in education.

Both films capture well youngsters trapped in a school system where they struggle to process. Like our example above they sit all day in classrooms where sound comes at them, but they cannot make sense of it in context.

They know teachers are speaking, but they cannot understand everything that is being said. This is interpreted by the school as being because they are not concentrating or listening, rather than they have a sound processing problem that needs addressing. Problems with the sound processing have also blocked their development of other skills such as motor skills and vision.

A full analysis of the film H is for Harry can be found on YouTube: https://www.youtube.com/watch?v=cDOE29OaAko&t=799s&ab_channel=Fit2Learn It is useful to watch the film too https://www.hisforharry.com/. As the film progresses observe changes in Harry's postural control, leaning off to one side, hence damaging his vision; and Harry's sense of despair. Eventually, Harry nudges the situation to bring it to an end. Harry was a bright young student, who really wanted to do well, but could not because he had various blocks to his processing, all of which could have been sorted out.

Person E

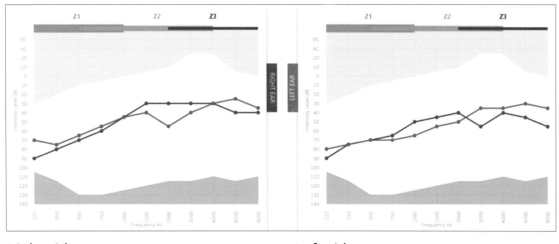

Right side   Left side

Client: Six-year-old struggling in education

What can be seen?

This is a shorter sound processing test for a younger child. We can see that the sound curves on both left and right sides are suppressed by up to 60 decibels at some points. The air (blue curve) and the bone (red curve) are clashing across the whole sound range. This child has probably experienced inner ear infection and still has some problems with keeping their airways clear.

So, a small child is desperately trying to engage in the world around them, but their speech is probably slurred or not well-developed for their age, and their ability to follow sounds like speech and singing is poor. They may be seen as having a poor attitude because they are not responding to instructions, but they genuinely cannot.

The objective has to be to get the sound curves on both sides working coherently without any confusion at all so that the child can function fully in all environments.

In order to move on this child needs to:

- Do sound therapy until all confusion on their sound processing has moved.
- Then it is important to also check that motor skills and vision are all properly developing as problems with sound processing can delay development in other areas.

Not all children are willing to cooperate...

Sometimes a child will not wear headphones to undertake sound therapy. There is no way forward without sorting out the sound processing.

Taking the child out for hours of physical activity until they are exhausted and ready to sleep deeply, even if they have headphones on, is a strategy that has worked well for many clients.

Alternatively, some children will accept bone conduction of sound through their spines more readily than headphones. It may be necessary to start slowly to get the child used to sound therapy before moving onto headphones.

Other children will happily wear headphones in a school environment, but not at home. Whilst others are happy to wear headphones whilst sitting on their mother's knee where they feel secure, but nowhere else.

Do whatever works to persuade the child to cooperate.

Also consider strategies to help the child establish good clear airways such as:

- Improving posture through exercises so that their Eustachian tube works more effectively.
- Teaching the child to breathe nasally so that they clear any nasal congestion every day until they have established a good breathing routine.

Person F

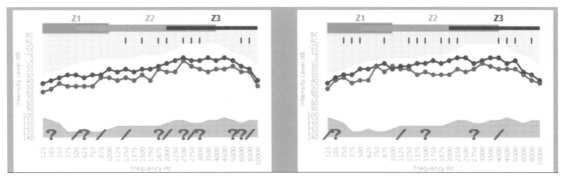

Right side   Left side

Client: Graduate in 20s struggling to access employment

What can be seen?

The blue marks along the top of the screenshots show the points at which the person struggles with pitch differentiation – i.e., they are not sure if one sound is higher or lower than another sound. That impacts on the person's ability to understand speech or written text in context. When working with the client it is worth listening to their speech and considering whether it is appropriate and in context.

The red marks along the bottom of the screenshots show the points where the person struggles to identify direction of sound on bone conduction. This is quite a problem on both sides, it is disrupting messages going from ear to brain.

On both sides the air conduction of sound is suppressed up to 20 decibels below the location of the ideal curve.

The air and bone conduction of sound do not work together coherently. There are points where the two curves clash and there are points where there are big gaps of more than 10 decibels between the two curves. Again, that disrupts the message going from ear to brain.

The two sides of the sound processing are sufficiently different that they do not work together coherently. Further, another sub-test has indicated that the person is struggling to follow sound when it moves and is left-ear dominant. Consequently, there is a microsecond delay on their sound processing, that is obviously slowing down reaction times.

Further conversation with the person reveals that they are:

- A highly qualified person who struggles to access or retain employment.
- Struggling with pitch differentiation which is causing problems with social engagement.

Visualise this person...

This person is academically very able, well they can pass examinations in their subject area. However, even though their skills are in a skills shortage area, they struggle to get employed or to keep employment.

They really struggle with the softer social skills. This also affects their personal life. When they speak to people they often bark out speech in a loud voice, in a monotone. People find this quite aggressive and offensive. Equally they fail to pick up on the mood or feelings of other people from their speech.

British comedy thrives on creating situations around such characters, however in real life it can be very difficult.

Moving on...

- The person needs to do sound therapy until they can make good sense of other people's speech.
- They may well also need to work on ensuring their facial muscles work well on both sides of their face.
- Also ensure that their binocular vision is working well and is integrated with their sound processing.
- Thus, in social encounters their sound, vision and motor skills in their face work together to make sense of situations and to respond and behave appropriately.

Person G

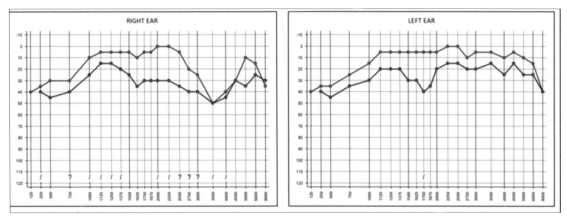

Right side   Left side

Client: Tradesman in 20s struggling with friendships and conflicts with employers

What can be seen?

It should be obvious to everyone that there is a massive dip in the sound processing curves on the right side on both air and bone conduction of sound. Also, a big dip on bone conduction (red curve) on the left side. The person had had a bad throat infection in their late teens/early 20s, e.g., something like glandular fever and this had left a huge impact on their sound processing skills.

It was not noticeable as a particular problem with speech and language, but it manifested in erratic confrontational behaviour with friends and employers. The person was up and down emotionally.

Dips in sound processing can destabilise a person emotionally. The dips can trigger depression. When the dips are moved the person becomes a lot more predictable and consistent in their behaviour and moods.

The person had had excellent development in all areas until the illness.

Moving on…

- The person needed to do sound therapy until both sides of sound processing were working together coherently and any dips were removed completely.
- That then supported the other senses and motor skills which were already in a good place.

Person H

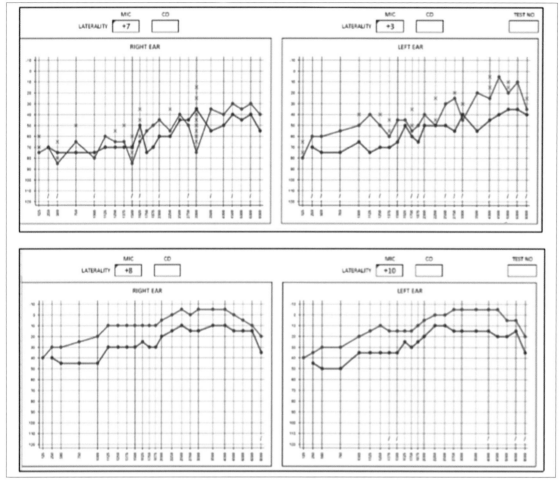

Right side   Left side

Client: Eight-year-old who struggled with speech and learning

What can be seen?

These are before and after shots of one round of sound therapy. At the start the child's sound processing was massively suppressed by up to 60 decibels. Also, there was huge confusion about the direction of sound on air marked with X and on bone conduction of sound marked with /. Further, he was left ear dominant and could not follow sound when it moved. His sound processing was severely compromised by the after-effects of inner ear infection.

In a classroom environment he could pick up very little of what was happening or understand the teacher's speech at all.

His own speech was slurred and difficult to understand, despite years of speech therapy.

His vision was quite closed and he only worked with the central 5% of his visual field. His motor skills, posture and gait were not well developed.

He had obviously had problems with inner ear infection on both left and right sides. That had restricted his global development.

One month later after 14 days of sound therapy...

- He was a completely changed child, he was now able to process most of the sounds around him.
- As a consequence, his social engagement was far more alert. He was proud of himself and no longer looked withdrawn.

However, be aware that delays in sound processing cause global delays, so he still had months of work to do to:

- Gain perfect sound processing curves.
- Gain full motor skills control.
- Gain binocular vision and to learn to process visually.
- Catch up on years of missed schoolwork.

But that was now all possible because the huge problems with sound processing were now largely removed.

Person I

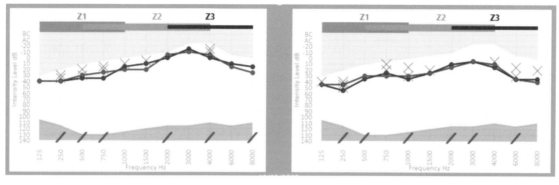

Right side   Left side

Client: Child of seven with significant dental decay

What can be seen?

This is a shorter reading of sound processing for a young child. There are fewer points checked, but it is clear that the sound processing is significantly confused.

The blue crosses (X) indicate points at which the child is confused about the direction of sound on air processing. When these are present the child really struggles to process anything in a classroom. Background noise and reverberation of sound in the class are very difficult for the child to deal with.

The air (blue curve) and the bone (red curve) conduction of sound on both sides are clashing across the whole sound range. This is further confusing messages going from ears to brain.

The red dashes at the bottom of the screen on both left and right sides indicates that the child is also confused about the direction of sound on bone conduction across much of the sound range.

The child's teeth are black, and the it has experienced significant dental decay. This in turn has inflamed the airways in the head and caused the child to be a mouth breather, rather than a nasal breather. The child is subject to recurrent bouts of inner ear infection.

There is little that sound therapy can do permanently until the various infections and blockages in the child's face and head are addressed. Once they are then it will be possible to remedy the current situation. In the meantime, the child is not able to process much in a school environment.

The child also has retained primitive reflexes so has poor postural control and understanding of left and right sides of their body.

When they were asked to draw the Tansley Figure ground shapes the child produced the following:

The shapes the child was trying to produce were as follows:

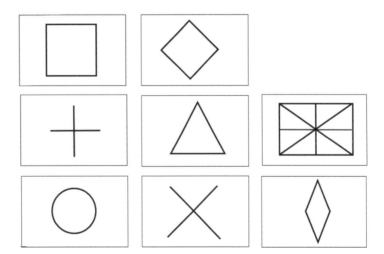

There are specific ages at which a child would be expected to be able to reproduce each of the shapes based on the Tansley Standard Figures: circle clockwise = three years; circle counterclockwise five years; cross = three and a quarter years; square = four years; X = four and a half to five and a half years; triangle = six years; diamond = seven to seven and a half years; Union Jack = six years.

The child's visual tracking skills were also checked and can be seen below.

The child is not skilled at using their eyes to focus on a fixed point, or to read numbers in large or small font text. The child's eyes do not work together, nor can they until the issues with primitive reflexes and sound processing are addressed.

Focusing on a fixed point   Reading large numbers   Reading small numbers

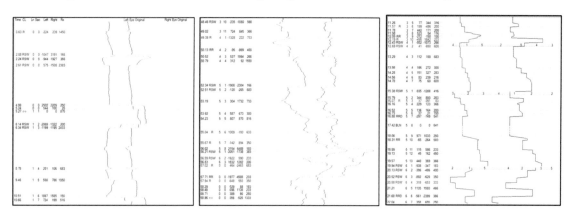

When the child read for meaning they tended to move their head and not their eyes and read aloud to themselves. The screenshots of the child's eye movements suggest that in order to read they are suppressing one eye, so in fact only reading with one eye. The child's understanding of what they had read was limited.

Reading for meaning

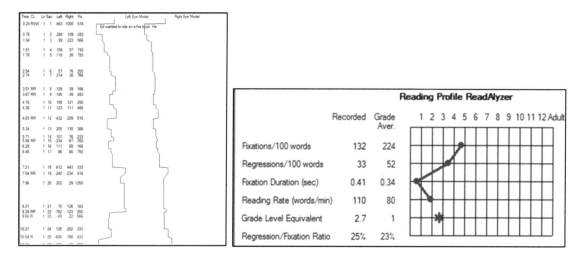

The child is working hard to please parents and teachers. But the child is not fit to learn. Pushing the child to learn with all these underlying issues without addressing them forces the child into relying on coping strategies for life; this is very stressful, so creates mental health problems. It also blocks good development. It can have an adverse effect on lifelong physical health.

Person J

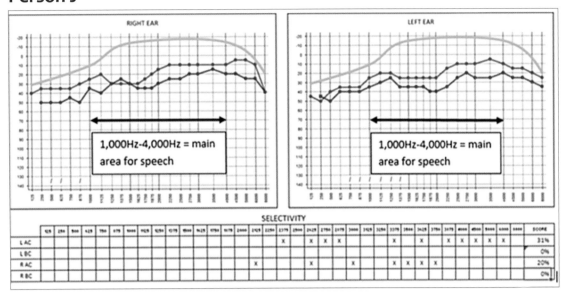

Right side   Left side

Client: Afro-Caribbean teenager excluded from school

Background

> "In 2018/19 fixed-term exclusions of black children made up 42 per cent of all exclusions in Croydon and permanent exclusions made up 39 per cent. But figures from the 2011 census show that just 20 per cent of the population in Croydon is black African, Caribbean or Black British. This means proportionately the number of exclusions of children from black ethnic backgrounds are double what they ought to be."
>
> Source: *South London News*

What can be seen?

Living in a hostile culture can be very difficult and can cause people to close down to survive. That can be seen in their sound processing curves. So, the area that is most suppressed for this boy is the area for language processing, alas that will also impact on his global development.

This boy's family also lived in private rented accommodation which kept the family insecure and stressed. They had spent some time living in emergency hostels. His parents were on low incomes, in insecure work.

The Afro-Caribbean community have to be understood in terms of the heritage of slavery, as well as racism. Like many brutalised communities the trauma is intergenerational. As we grow up, we develop our ability to stay calm through coregulation with our parents, but if our parents are habitually stressed or have no heritage of calm parenting, that is very difficult.

Schools with very rigid disciplinary policies compound these issues by not responding appropriately to the needs of the parents and the children.

Further, narratives are created around the children based on very flimsy evidence by schools and social workers. Even when schools are presented with a full analysis of the child's cognitive processing, they will not support the child to feel secure or to access their basic skills. The child then feels further rejection and a sense that no matter what they do they cannot please the school.

The child's conclusion is fully documented in their sound curves – they just shut down. It is safer, but in the long-term it restricts their lifetime opportunities. Consequently, for this youngster we could also see that his eye tracking skills were immature, and he struggled with motor skills development, particularly crossing his mid-line.

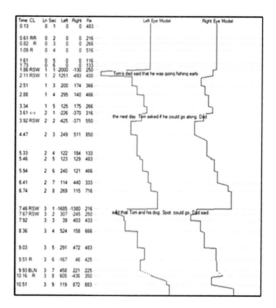 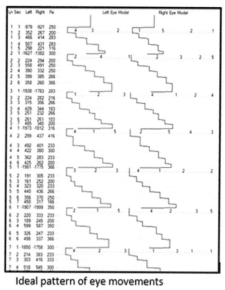

Ideal pattern of eye movements

The youngsters eye tracking movements were captured using eye tracking technology and can be seen in the box on the left. Compare the eye movements to those on the right. The youngster's eyes did not work together to send messages efficiently from eye to brain. Suppressed sound processing and erratic eye movements will have made reading for meaning a frustrating task.

The youngster needs constructive support so that he can develop a full range of cognitive skills. All that he will be offered are coping strategies such as tutoring that assume that sound processing, visual processing and motor skills development are all in place. Theories of "mindset" project failure back on to the young person, which exacerbates the underlying problems.

Person K

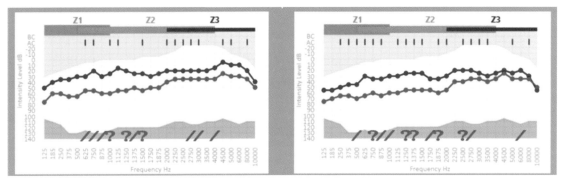

Right side   Left side

Client: Adult dyslexic

What can be seen?

This person has multiple problems with their sound processing. They are left-ear dominant so there is a delay on their sound processing. Further, the blue dashes along the top of the screenshots indicate that this person struggles to identify changes in pitch, this will impact on their understanding of subtleties in speech when it is both written and spoken.

There are significant differences on sound processing on both air (blue curve) and bone (red curve) on left and right sides. The air and bone conduction curves do not run together with a consistent gap of 10 decibels.

All of these issues will disrupt efficient sound processing from ear to brain and back.

In addition, this person has retained reflexes which mean that their eyes jump when they cross the mid-line. This affects all tasks that involve working across the mid-line or understanding any concept as a whole. The problems can be seen when a person is asked to make a 12-piece jigsaw and they struggle to bring both sides of the puzzle together.

Further, when the eye movements were observed the person's eye movements were relatively regular when reading numbers in small font text. However, when the person was asked to read for meaning, the eye movements became dysregulated. Reading for meaning requires a person to bring together sound and vision. In the case this person their right eye stopped altogether at some points.

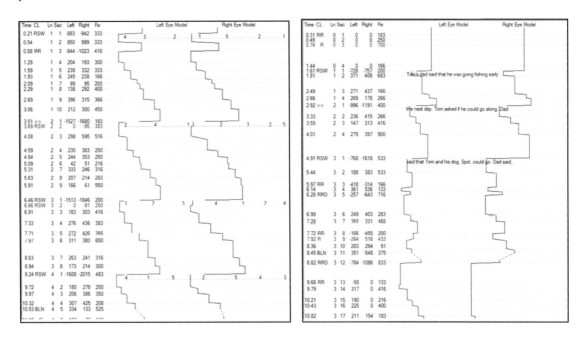

Consider how hard it is for this person to read for meaning:

(a)   Their sound processing is confused and delayed.
(b)   They struggle to cross their mid-line which impacts on their understanding of concepts as a whole and causes their eyes to jump at the mid-line.
(c)   Their eye movements are disrupted by the problems with sound processing.

Imagine then having to work in a noisy classroom or office environment. Life will be exhausting for this person.

Such blocks to so many aspects of cognitive processing wear people out and cause them to feel hyper-alert. That in turn can trigger mental health problems.

Coping strategies might allow a person to jump through various exams, but they are not always useful in real life. If possible, it is kinder to empower people for life with a full range of skills in terms of motor skills, sound processing, binocular vision and visual processing.

Person L

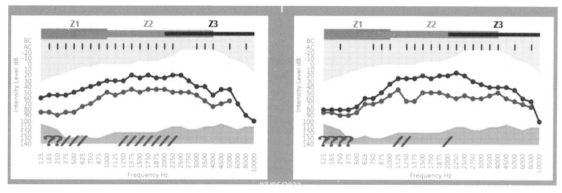

Right side   Left side

Client: Long-term unemployed mature adult with low skills, subject to a benefits sanction

Background

"Benefit sanctions are in effect punishment fines whereby claimants' social security benefits are docked for at least a month for supposed infringements, such as failing to search for jobs or missing a meeting with an employment coach.... Government Ministers have claimed sanctions focus the minds of claimants on work discipline, while the weight of academic evidence shows they are ineffective and much more likely to make people impoverished, unwell and less likely to work."

Guardian, March 2023

What can be seen?

The person has probably experienced severe inner ear infection in their infancy. This has impacted on their lifetime skills development and restricted and confused their sound processing for their whole life.

Their struggles with pitch differentiation across the whole sound range mean that they always have difficulties understanding speech in context and responding appropriately to spoken responses by others, be they family members, potential employers or government officials. They do not have any conscious control over this confusion and need sound therapy to help them move on.

Problems with sound processing can impact on a person's ability to sequence and to manage time. Sound processing that is as confused as this person's is going to make it very hard for them to comply with a strict regime that requires them to meet precise targets.

The person needs to be made to feel safe so that they can use all their senses as far as possible and respond to any therapies offered.

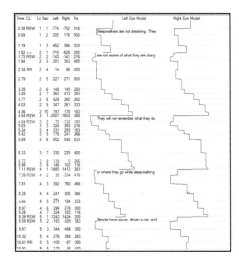

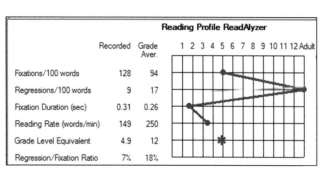

When we looked at this person's eye movements when reading for meaning, we could see that the eyes worked in some sort of pattern, but aspects of their reading were at a primary school level. The time it took the person to focus on a section of text, the fixation duration, was 0.31 seconds – too slow to read properly. Their reading speed was 149wpm. Anything below 200wpm is not considered to be functional literacy. The comprehension score indicated that the person had little recall of what they have just read.

This person's problems were predominantly related to sound processing. The solution therefore is to address their sound processing.

This person was genuinely desperate to go to work and engage in adult life as a full citizen. Sanctioning them just made them frightened and feel unsafe, so they could not move on.

5

Checking and maintaining your own sound processing skills for life

Speech and language games to build sound processing skills

The connection between primitive reflexes and sound processing

Checking your own sound processing skills

Sound processing and sound therapy are relatively new areas of therapy. It is not a medical intervention; it is a way of exercising muscles in the middle ear and thus agitating the vestibular system.

Sound is a person's first sense, and it impacts on many areas of the body. Our ears work 24/7 and are our first point of alertness to any threat from the outside world, and subsequently may engage either the parasympathetic or sympathetic nervous system.

A qualified Tomatis sound consultant can assess your sound processing skills and help you understand the sound curves. When you choose a sound therapist it is important that you choose one that is going to provide you with the sort of detailed analysis we have seen in the case studies.

You can find a Tomatis sound therapist near you if you look on the Tomatis website: www.tomatis.com

You can also find details of how to train in Tomatis sound therapy on the website.

There are some clinics offering their own "in-house sound therapy" which they have designed. Take care, ensure that any sound therapy will have the following features:

- Uses air and bone conduction of sound.
- Music which is filtered and gated.
- Assessments which are clear, which will regularly track your progress.
- Research studies in that specific therapy.
- International recognition.

How often should a person check their sound processing skills?

In an ideal world every seven- or eight-year-old should be screened for sound processing skills so that any problems can be quickly addressed.

It is a good idea to check again before a child enters high school, just to ensure that there are no obvious issues that would make a move to a much more demanding environment difficult.

A further check at 16 or 17 years of age would make sense to ensure that the transition through puberty has not unsettled the person's basic functioning; and that they are in good shape to face public examinations.

Then throughout life perhaps once a decade, people should check their sound processing skills and ensure that they are secure. This is particularly important if the person experiences any big changes or shocks in life.

Sound therapy can be particularly useful to women going through pregnancy, and to the developing infant.

At around 50 years old everyone should have a thorough preventative health check-up. A key part of that is ensuring that sound processing is working well as loss of sound is known to be a key indicator of Alzheimer's. As sound therapy impacts on many areas of physical and cognitive function, it is a good thing to do to maintain senses, and confidence in areas such as balance, navigation and motor skills.

Sound therapy tools can be used throughout life to accelerate learning in many areas, such as:

- Memorising course notes
- Learning to sing
- Learning a new language
- Fine-tuning public speaking skills
- Boosting overall concentration skills
- Shaking off trauma
- Resetting your global systems after a trying day

Speech and language games to build sound processing skills

1. As well as doing passive sound therapy it is a good idea to do active work with sound processing. This should include work with sound therapy using an audio-vocal loop, such as a Forbrain (https://www.forbrain.com), or the microphone on an infinite headset, or to learn English as a foreign language using a pronounce device https://pronounce.com . A good example of active language work can be found on YouTube
https://www.youtube.com/watch?v=0_HfQ2TEjfk&ab_channel=PRONOUNCEEnglish
There Thibaut Bosworth Gerome provides a very wide range of stimulus for people learning English as a second language. It is also useful material for native English speakers who have gaps in their language learning.

There are lots of sound games that can be played by people in pairs or in groups. Such games include:

- **I went to market.** In this game the first person states: "I went to market, and I bought and names an item (e.g., a bear or a bag of sweets or a car, anything). The second person then states: "I went to market, and I bought" and lists the first item plus an additional item. The game goes on until someone fails to remember all the items bought in the market.
- **Describing an object** without mentioning the name of the object. The rest of the people have to guess the item.
- **I spy with my little eye.** In this game a person sees an item but does not tell anyone and says "I spy with my little eye something beginning with (the person names the letter at the start of the word that they are thinking of)". The other people guess what the word could be until they guess right. Then the winner selects the next word.
- **Twenty questions.** One player thinks of a random item and tells the others whether it could be classified as animal, mineral or vegetable. The other players have twenty questions in which to ask the first person about the item and try to guess what the item is. The first player only answers yes or no.

2. **Playing Theatre Sports.** These are short drama games which require the players to improvise. There are many such examples and they are a lot of fun and quite silly. Many such games can easily be found online if you search for "Theatres Sports Games". Examples include:

- **Three Lines** – An exercise to train scene start-ups. Two players initiate a scene; the scene is broken off after three lines. The goal is to establish as much as possible as fast as possible. We want to understand the characters, the environment and the points of view of the characters. Once three lines of dialogue have been uttered, restart a different scene.

- **Actor Switch** – A scene is started, played by two players. Mid-scene the organiser interrupts, and all characters are replaced by new players. The new players should take over the original characters and stick to the story that was being developed.

- **Distance Game** – Two players stand a few feet apart facing each other and have the most boring four-line interchange possible. They then without telling each other pick a specific distance they want to be from the other person and repeat the interchange while maintaining the distance. The maintaining of distance automatically seems to affect people's emotional commitment and inflection. The key is to have a specific distance in mind down to the centimetre. If one person picks one metre but the other picks ten centimetres, you will see some interesting conflict because of that difference in distances chosen.

3. **Recite and memorise poems or famous speeches.** Once a person starts doing this regularly they soon observe a significant improvement in their auditory recall, especially if they incorporate use of sound therapy equipment.

This can be further strengthened by including hand clapping or rhythmic tapping activities at the same time. This helps integrate sound and motor skills.

4. **Speech and language games** that take a bit of thought...

- **Rhyming words:** The first person says a word, e.g., "tin" and the other players have to think of as many words as they can that rhyme with "tin". The winner chooses the next starter word.

- **Swapping words:** Read a simple familiar story sentence by sentence and get the players to think of ways to swap the words in the sentence. For example, the phrase "Each peach pear plum I spy Tom Thumb" might be swapped to "Each peach pear plum I spy a big sum".

- **Cropping words:** This game involves a person calling out words and asking the other person to say it with one syllable. For example, "I say superman, now you say without the super" and the correct reply would be "man". Below are some suggested words to get you going.

a.   I say "basketball, now you say without the "basket". (ball)

b.   I say "snapdragon", now you say without the "snap". (dragon)

c.   I say "napkin", now you say without the "nap". (kin)

d.   I say "misfit", now you say without the "mis". (fit)

e.   I say "cabin", now you say without the "cab". (in)

Word bank of possible words for this game: campus, unfit, nutmeg, attic, camping, robin, talcum, magnet, bellman, catnip, shellfish, nutshell, cannot, gunship, sunlit, hotbed, setup, pitfall, within, hubcap, sunbath, bedpan, catnap, backspin.

- The game can be reversed, and the person is asked to say the word without the second syllable. For example, "I say superman now you say without the man". (super).
- **Phoneme changing games.** The players start with one simple word, for example "lit" and take it in turns to change one syllable. Thus, the word might change from lit, to sit. to sat, to cat, to cot, to hot and so on.

The connection between primitive reflexes and sound processing

Primitive reflexes are involuntary reflex actions that originate in the central nervous system. They are exhibited in all infants without disabilities but should not be present in older children or adults. The development of the prefrontal lobes, as a baby transitions into infancy, should cause these reflexes to be integrated into other movement patterns.

In modern times it is not unusual for older children and adults to retain these reflexes, which can inhibit their vestibular and sensory integration development.

Most primitive reflexes should be integrated by 12 months, although a few will normally be present until three and a half years of age.

Dr Alfred Tomatis observed that the ear (sound processing) plays an important role in posture, balance and muscular tone. Sound is an important trigger to assist with an infant's global development.

Several factors are blocking the full integration of primitive reflexes in modern life, such as inner ear infection in infants under three years old which deafens them for a period and removes the stimulus for movement; also, restraints on infants' movements such as being in chairs of one form or another for extended periods; also anything that disturbs a calm natural birth.

It is a two-way process: if motor skills are addressed, then sound processing is improved and vice versa. If both sound and motor skills therapies are used, then there are synergies.

$$2 + 2 = 5$$

Synergies are when two inputs create a greater output than the sum of the parts.

If there have been problems with sound and motor skills development then there will also be problems with full development of visual skills. Vision is our last sense to develop and needs a platform of motor skills and sound processing to be in place in order to function fully.

Postural control

There are some primitive reflexes which particularly support good postural control. Ensuring these are integrated and maintained will have a positive impact on sound processing.

Spinal galant reflex

The spinal galant reflex is the reflex at the base of the spine in an infant that when touched, triggers a desire to urinate and defecate. This is useful in a new-born infant, but as the child develops normally, they should gain control of their bladder and bowel muscles. If this does not happen, the child will keep triggering this reflex every time anything touches the base of their spine. This makes them a very wriggly child, consequently, this can be confused for attention deficit hyperactivity disorder.

The spinal galant reflex needs to be integrated for the muscles supporting the spine to develop properly. Where the reflex is present on one side only, it can cause scoliosis, as the muscles along the spine do not develop equally on both sides.

The exercises to address this issue can be found in our Developing Motor Skills book or online on our YouTube channel: https://www.youtube.com/watch?v=lyvrlaaDELY&t=197s&ab_channel=Fit2Learn

Tonic labyrinth reflex

The tonic labyrinth reflex (TLR) involves the vestibular system in the inner ear and how it integrates with other senses and balance. TLR is triggered when the head is tipped backwards or forwards, influencing the tone in the front and back parts of the body, and eye movements up and down. This ensures that the body's balance can be maintained at all times.

The TLR forward pattern emerges in utero, should be fully developed at birth, and should integrate at approximately four months of life. The TLR backward pattern emerges at birth and can begin integrating as early as three months and as late as three years of age.

The exercises to address this issue can be found in our *Developing Motor Skills* book or online on our YouTube channel: https://www.youtube.com/watch?v=ol6Sx8xHG1M&t=64s&ab_channel=Fit2Learn

Symmetric tonic neck reflex

The symmetric tonic neck reflex helps infants to use the top half and the bottom half of their body independently of each other and in coordinated moves. This is important for:

- Posture
- Focus
- Hand–eye coordination

The exercises to address this issue can be found in our *Developing Motor Skills* book or online on our YouTube channel: https://www.youtube.com/watch?v=id9wHaNlTEM&ab_channel=Fit2Learn

Maintaining good core strength and posture for life

Even when primitive reflexes are integrated, everyone should proactively work on maintaining core strength and upright posture. In our experience children need to be supported and encouraged throughout their school lives or they will soon slip back into slumped postures.

Likewise adults need work and home environments and lifestyles which encourage good postural control. Most people need community support to encourage them to maintain their basic fitness.

Other factors that commonly affect postural control

Psoas region

The psoas region is the area around the hips and the top of the thighs. It is a major junction in the human body and if the hips are not quite in the right position this can place huge pressure on the nervous system and make a person anxious. It can also disrupt postural control.

The psoas region

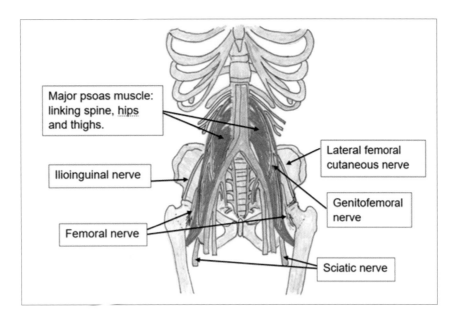

The nerves and muscles in this region connect the legs, the hips and the spine. It is an important area that needs to be established and maintained.

In our *Developing Motor Skills* book, we recommend that people do (a) the squashed frog exercise (page 13) and (b) Pelvic Tilts exercise (page 52) to bring the hips into alignment.

The book: *The Vital Psoas Muscle* by Jo Ann Staugaard-Jones is a good practical book which provides detailed explanations of how to support this area.

Feet

Our feet are the foundations of our adult frame. Feet impact on all aspects of how the skeletal frame works, hence are very important for postural control.

Feet develop better if children are allowed to spend as much time as possible moving about in bare feet.

Humans are born with flat feet and develop arches throughout childhood. Research suggests that the optimal age range for arch development is four to six years old and that arches are usually formed completely by age eight. (Lincolnshire NHS)

A useful book to discover more about the development of feet is *Finding Their Feet* by Bernie Landels (2022).

Vision

Good focusing skills support good posture, and good posture supports the development of good focusing skills. When a person habitually adjusts their posture to gain a better focus, or to close off one eye and work with the other eye, then that will impact on a person's postural control.

It is therefore vital that as far as possible everyone achieves good balanced binocular vision and visual processing skills.

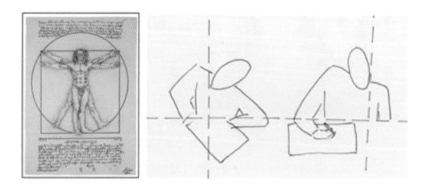

Mid-line crossing

There are some primitive reflexes that support mid-line crossing skills. Ensuring that these are integrated and maintained will have a positive impact on sound processing.

When mid-line crossing is not well established it can cause overflow around the neck, mouth and jaw that puts pressure on the nerves in those areas and can trigger tinnitus, migraines and Tourette's syndrome. Any habitual pressure in these areas will compromise sound processing skills. Mid-line crossing issues can also manifest in terms of habitual rapid blinking.

Asymmetric tonic neck reflex

The asymmetric tonic neck reflex is the primitive reflex that needs to be integrated in order to allow the head to turn to either side without the body also moving.

If this does not integrate, then it causes the eyes to jump every time they cross the mid-line. This disrupts eye-tracking skills and therefore reading and writing skills.

From a sound point of view, it causes overflow around the jaw area as people struggle to work with left and right hand, eye and brain. That tightening around the jaw area compromises the cranial nerves that connect the ear and the jaw muscles.

In order to get sound processing working properly and fully, people need to integrate this reflex and learn to relax their jaw, see page 45.

The exercises to address this issue can be found in our *Developing Motor Skills* book or online on our YouTube channel: https://www.youtube.com/watch?v=Of2vhFMZvBY&t=418s&ab_channel=Fit2Learn

Moro reflex

The Moro reflex is the reflex that triggers the fight, flight, freeze response in infants. Infants are helpless and they need to quickly alert parents and carers that help is needed or that they feel unsafe.

As children develop, they do not need to be hyper-alert. However, many children continue to be shy, timid and anxious and some are selective mutes and rarely feel confident enough to speak with anyone beyond their close circle.

Integrating this reflex has many benefits:

- It causes the larynx to drop lower in the trachea, this makes speaking and swallowing feel much more comfortable. Thus, the person is able to develop more confident speech and does not feel like they are being strangled in a formal setting.
- When the larynx is in the right place, then the vocal cords do not scissor (rub) against each other. When the vocal cords scissor, it can trigger growths (polyps) on the vocal cords.
- A person's sense of left and right improves as they gain conscious control of their left and right limbs. This in turn impacts on their navigational skills.

The exercises to address this issue can be found in our *Developing Motor Skills* book (https://fit-2-learn.com/publications/) or online on our YouTube channel: https://www.youtube.com/watch?v=iA7ExcwS-M0&t=40s&ab_channel= Fit2Learn

Going on to master mid-line crossing.

If a person misses stages in their development such that there are problems with mid-line crossing, then it is important to go back and address those issues.

Sorting out primitive reflexes and eye movements is not enough to ensure that a person six years+ is working across their mid-line in their brain, as well. To build mid-line crossing skills it is useful to do various activities which promote working across the mid-line, for example juggling without moving the head and the body.

Fit 2 Learn have created a set of resources and a manual to support developing children's and adults mid-line crossing skills. (https://fit-2-learn.com/shop/)

Appendices

* Nursery rhymes, poems and songs for children up to eight years old

* D.B. Harmon's studies

* Glossary of terms

* References and further reading

* Sound and vision working together

* Conditions associated with problems with sound processing systems

* Useful websites and contact details

Nursery rhymes, poems and songs for children up to eight years old

All of these nursery rhymes, poems and songs have been chosen to encourage movement, rhythm, speech and language development. Ideally children will associate the rhymes with jumping around reciting and enjoying language. In five to ten years' time these skills will develop into good writing skills, but first the children need to develop spoken language skills. The rhymes can all be found online.

Traditional Nursery Rhymes	Pattercake, Pattercake, Baker's Man
The Grand Old Duke of York	Early to Bed and Early to Rise
Incy, Wincy Spider	It's Raining, It's Pouring
Jack And Jill	This is the Way We Wash Our Hands
Little Bo Peep	Sing a Song of Sixpence
Mary, Mary Quite Contrary	Horsey, Horsey Don't You Stop
Diddle, Diddle, Dumpling My Son John	One Two Buckle My Shoe
Doctor Foster Went to Gloucester	A Ring-A-Ring-A-Roses
Little Jack Horner	Ride a Cock Horse toBanbury Cross
Little Miss Muffet	Girls and Boys Come Out To Play
Old Mother Hubbard	
Wee Willie Winkie	
Baa Baa Black Sheep	**Poems**
Hickety Pickety My Black Hen	This Is the House That Jack Built (Anon)
Hickory Dickory Dock	Now We Are Six (A.A. Milne)
Ladybird, Ladybird	The Owl and the Pussycat (E. Lear)
Mary Had a Little Lamb	On the Ning Nang Nong (S. Milligan)
The Lion and The Unicorn	The Purple Cow (G. Burgess)
Three Blind Mice	My Shadow (R.L. Stevenson)
Oranges and Lemons	Peas (Anon)
Two Little Dicky Birds	If All the World Were Paper (Anon)
Rub-A-Dub-Dub, Three Men in a Tub	Please Mrs Butler (A. Ahlberg)
This Little Piggy	Little Red Riding Hood and the Wolf (R. Dahl)
Humpty Dumpty	The King's Breakfast (A.A. Milne)
Jack Be Nimble	Spaghetti! Spaghetti! (J. Prelutsky)
Goosey, Goosey Gander	Green Eggs and Ham (Dr Seuss)
Little Boy Blue	The Song of the Train (D. McCord)
One For Sorrow	The Jumblies (E. Lear)
I Had a Little Nut Tree	The Ceremonial Band (J. Reeves)
Girls and Boys Come Out to Play	The Song of the Jellicles (T.S. Eliot)
Hot Cross Buns	The Quangle Wangle's Hat (E. Lear)
	The Spider And The Fly (M. Howitt)

Jamaica Market (A. Maxwell-Hall)
Rules (B. Patten)
Please Do Not Feed the Animals (R. Hull)
Anger (J. Joster)
Billy McBone (A. Ahlberg)
Cat-Rap (G. Nichols)
Crick, Crack, Crocodile (J. Poulson)
Growing (T. Mitton)
Harry the Hamster (C. Gittins)
Ten Dancing Dinosaurs (J. Foster)
The Boneyard Rap (W. Magee)
Variation on an Old Nursery Rhyme (J, Mole)
The Paint Box (E.V. Rieu)
A Smile (J. Alborough)
Bad Day At The Ark (R. McGough)
The Magic Box (K. Wright)
I Am Falling Off a Mountain (J. Prelutsky)
Elephant Walking (C. Sansom)
My Grannies (P. Corbett)
Busy Day (M. Rosen)

Songs
One, Two, Three, Four, Five
Old MacDonald Had a Farm
Ten in the Bed
Polly Put the Kettle On
There's a Hole in the Bucket
Row, Row, Row Your Boat
Five Little Monkeys Jumping on the Bed
Bobby Shafto
Oats and Beans and Barley Grow
Here We Go Round the Mulberry Bush
Lavender's Blue
Dance to Your Daddy
London Bridge is Falling Down
London's Burning
Twinkle, Twinkle, Little Star
Head, Shoulders, Knees and Toes
I Am the Music man and I Come From Down Your Way

Happy Birthday
How Much is That Doggy in the Window
I am H.A.P.P.Y.
There Was an Old Man Called Michael Finnegan
The Court of King Caractacus
One Finger One Thumb Keep Moving
Aiken Drum
Ten Green Bottles
One Man Went to Mow
The Big Ship Sails on The Ally Ally Oh
The Animal Fair
The Animals Went in Two By Two
The Hokey-Cokey
I Can Sing a Rainbow
If You Are Happy and You Know it
They Was an Old Lady Who Swallowed a Fly
She'll Be Coming Round the Mountain
Oh Jemima
Go and Tell Aunt Nancy
Kookaburra
Yankee Doodle
Skip To My Lou

D.B. Harmon's Studies

In the 1940s, D.B. Harmon established that children learn and breathe better if they sit with good posture. He screened over 160,000 children and identified that 20% of children entered school with visual problems, and that after five years of education 80% of children had visual problems. They had also developed postural problems.

We know from the work of Dr Alfred Tomatis that poor posture will compromise good sound processing.

Harmon recommended that ideally children should be sitting with good posture to read and that the text should be angled at 22 degrees. This would enable them to read without refocusing their eyes for every line of text, and to breathe with an open windpipe.

Harmon's studies can be downloaded for no charge from the internet. He also considered light and the angle children sit at to the board.

The Society of Teachers of the Alexander Technique are currently campaigning for school furniture to be better designed to prevent a range of postural problems in young people. They are particularly concerned about flat desks and backward sloping chairs.

The link to their campaign can be found on this website: http://www.alexander.ie/chairscampaign.html

Their campaign video is on this link:
https://www.youtube.com/watch?v=f3AL5SK_tUI&t=155s

Glossary of Terms

Bilateral Integration is the process of getting the left side of the body to work smoothly with the right side of the body and vice versa. This is an indicator that the left and right sides of the brain are communicating and sharing information efficiently.

Core Strength refers to the muscles that support your core and those that keep the body upright. Core strength is not fully developed until seven or eight years of age and will fluctuate as the child grows. Until that age children struggle to control posture and complete a cognitive task simultaneously.

Cranial Nerves refer to the twelve pairs of nerves emerging from the back of the brain. The nerves send electric messages to and from the head, neck and torso. They are a key part of the nervous system and help people to hear, see, taste, touch and move their facial muscles. Each nerve is paired and present on both sides of the body.

Fine Motor Skills refer to control of the intricate movements of the hands, the fingers, the face, the toes. For example, winking the eyes, smiling, pouting, holding a pen, doing up buttons, wriggling toes.

Gross Motor Skills refer to the control of the big muscles in the human body. That is the muscles in the arms and legs and the muscles that support the core and keep the body upright. Gross motor skills control needs to be in place in order for a child to properly develop fine motor skills control. Rushing straight to fine motor skills control will restrict the proper development of gross motor skills, which will in turn impact on sound processing skills.

Gross motor skills should be developed fully between the ages of six and eight years of age. They then need to be maintained properly for life.

Heart Rate Variance is the timing between successive heart beats. The heart is the most powerful beat in the body; if the heart rate is erratic it releases cortisol to the brain which triggers the brain to go into fight or flight. The heart rate can be trained to maintain a steady, smooth rhythm through learning to breathe smoothly and rhythmically and focusing on a happy thought.

Mid-line Crossing is the imaginary line down the centre of the body, which divides the body into left and right. This links with bilateral integration, both of which are integral with coordinated movements, allowing a person to be able to move their body, not just opposing left and right sides, but to be able to cross the central point of the body (mid-line). For example, being able to draw a horizontal line from left to right without swapping hands in the middle. Or moving their body to avoid mid-line crossing. Good development of mid-line crossing impacts on both sound and vision processing.

Primitive Reflexes are the involuntary reflex actions that originate in the central nervous system. They are exhibited in infants without disabilities; they should not be present in older children or adults. Thea development of the frontal lobes as a baby transitions into infancy should cause these reflexes to be integrated into other movement patterns. Sometimes older children and adults can retain these reflexes, which can greatly impact on their vestibular and sensory integration. This impacts on learning.

Most primitive reflexes have integrated by 12 months of age, although the tonic labyrinth reflex is still present until three and a half years of age.

Proprioception is the ability to sense stimuli from the body in terms of position, motion and balance. The sense comes from perception, usually subconsciously. This sense comes primarily from sensory nerve terminals and tendons, combined with vestibular processing.

Rhythm is a strong regular repeated pattern of sound or movement. Rhythm and music are important for learning sequences, movement, mathematical skills, and complex language. These are foundation skills.

Sound Processing is the ability to make sense of a sound as well as hear it. Sound processing is a complex process that starts in the first few weeks of life. A hearing test does not indicate whether a person can process sound, just that they can hear it. In order for a person to be able to process and make sense of sound there are a whole range of factors to understand.

Vestibular System links motor skills, sound and vision processing. The vestibular system is in the inner ear. It is this system that causes problems with balance, vertigo, travel sickness and so on.

Visual processing is the ability to identify, interpret and understand what is seen, which is learned and developed from birth. All children need the opportunity to learn and to work with two eyes perfectly together. We do not need "two perfect eyes", just "two eyes working perfectly together". Visual skills build and develop as we grow.

References and Further Reading

Sound Processing

1. The Ear and the Voice, Dr Alfred Tomatis, 2005
2. The Ear and Language, Dr Alfred Tomatis, 1996
3. Hearing Equals Behaviour, Dr Guy Berard & Sally Brockett, 2011
4. The Vestibular System, Goldberg et al, 2012
5. This is Your Brain on Music, Daniel Levitin, 2006
6. The World in Six Songs, How the Musical Brain Created Human Nature, Daniel Levitin, 2019
7. Not Just Talking, Siobhan Boyce, 2014
8. Train Your Brain to Hear, Jennifer Holland, 2014
9. Learn to Sing Learn to Read, Audrey Wisbey, 1981
10. The Universal Sense, How Hearing Shapes the Mind, Dr Seth S Horowitz, 2012
11. Physics and Music, the Science of Musical Sound, White and White, 1980
12. Comparing Notes:, How we make sense of music, Ockelford, 2017
13. The Power of Sound, Joshua Leeds, 2010
14. Music Cognition, The basics, Henkjan Honing, 2022
15. The Science of Music, How Technology has Shaped an Artform, May, 2023
16. An Individual Note of Music Sound and Electronics, Daphne Oram, 2016
17. LISTEN to LIVE – our Brain and Music: The Tomatis Listening training and therapy, Martien de Voigt and Józef Vervoort, 2018
18. Bridging Audiology and Psychology – The Secrets of the Auditory System – Carlos Alós, 2020

Breathing and Heart Rate Variance

1. Breath, James Nestor, 2020
2. The Dental Diet, Dr Steve Lin, 2018
3. Coherence, Dr Alan Watkins, 2012

Motor Skills Development

1. The Rhythmic Movement Method. Dr Harald Blomberg, 2015
2. Beyond the Sea Squirt, Moira Dempsey, 2019
3. Motor Control, Shumway-Cook & Woollacott, 2017

4. The Vital Psoas Muscles, Staugaard-Jones, 2012
5. The Maze of Learning, Motor Skills Development, Davies, Smith & Healy, 2018
6. Finding Their Feet, Landels, 2022

Vision and Visual Processing

1. Optometric Management of Learning-Related Vision Problems, Scheiman & Rouse, 1994
2. Improve Your Vision, Dr Steven Beresford et al, 1996

Sleep

1. Life Time, Russel Foster, 2022
2. Why We Sleep, Matthew Walker, 2017

Diet

1. Diet for the Mind, Dr Martha Clare Morris, 2017
2. Brain Food, Dr Lisa Mosconi, 2018
3. The Dental Diet, Dr Steve Lin, 2018

Motor-sensory Integration

1. Sensory Integration and the Child, Dr Jean Ayres, 2005
2. Piaget's Theory in Practice, Thinking Goes to School, Furth & Wachs, 1975
3. The Co-ordinated Classroom, D.B. Harmon, 1951
4. The Brain's Way of Healing, Norman Doidge, 2015
5. Thinking, Fast and Slow, Daniel Kahneman, 2011
6. The Genius in All of Us, David Shenk, 2010
7. The Woman Who Changed Her Brain, Barbara Arrowsmith-Young, 2012

Biological Anthropology – this is important because modern humans are de-evolving, and this is the framework for much of our work. Modern lifestyles and diet are creating an epidemic of health issues.

1. The Secret of Our Success, Joseph Henrich, 2016
2. The Story of the Human Body, Daniel Lieberman, 2013
3. The Evolution of the Human Head, Daniel Lieberman, 2011

Trauma – trauma affects every aspect of the body, so when we are working on any part of the body, we are thinking about helping the person move on from trauma and anxiety, if relevant.

1. Trauma is Really Strange, Steve Haines, 2015
2. The Body Keeps the Score, Bessel van der Kolk, 2015
3. Shake It Off Naturally, Dr David Berceli, 2015
4. The Polyvagal Theory, Stephen Porges, 2011
5. The Polyvagal Theory in Therapy – Engaging the Rhythm of Regulation, Deborah A. Dana and Stephen W. Porges, 2018

Sound and vision working together

It makes sense to be aware of how to maintain the muscles around the eyes and good focusing skills. In recent years there has been a significant increase in the number of people wearing visual aids such as glasses and contact lenses. Every school and workplace should be organising eye exercises for all of their community to help them maintain good eye health and prevent visual problems caused by modern work environments.

Vision exercises

1. Learn to wink with both eyes

2. Squeeze eyes tightly closed count to ten; open eyes very wide look around without moving head

3.  Moves to the left and to the right x 10

4. Move eyes up and down x 10

5. Move eyes in circles clockwise x 5

6. Move eyes in circles anti-clockwise x 5

7. Imagine that there is a big clock in front of you.... look at the centre, then move eyes out to one; then back to the centre; out to two; then back to the centre and so on until 12.

8. Converge and diverge eyes whilst focusing on a pencil top and keeping the pencil top as one single image. Keep practising daily until able to bring the top to your nose without going into double vision.

Converged eyes

9. Crossing the mid-line do this exercise **once the primitive reflexes are established:** using two pots at about shoulder width apart, patch one eye. Pick up items from pot A with left hand, move in an arc at eye height across mid-line and place in pot B continue until pot A is empty; still using the left hand return the items in the same manner to pot A; repeat with the right hand.

Patch the other eye and repeat. All the time that items are being moved from one pot to another the eye should be following the items.

Conditions associated with problems with sound processing systems

Motion sickness

Motion sickness occurs when a person's sound, vision and motor skills do not send their brain messages coherently enough for them to cope with rapid changes in position, such as travelling in a car or on a boat.

This can make a person feel nauseous.

Sound therapy and agitation of the vestibular system commonly resolves this problem.

Benign paroxysmal positional vertigo

Benign paroxysmal positional vertigo (BPPV) occurs when small pieces of bone-like calcium, canaliths, break free and float inside small canals in the inner ear. This sends confusing messages to the brain about the body's position, which causes vertigo.

The Epley manoeuvre is used to move the canaliths out of the canals, so they stop causing symptoms.

To perform the manoeuvre, your health care provider will:

- Turn your head toward the side that causes vertigo.
- Quickly lay you down on your back with your head in the same position just off the edge of the table. You will likely feel more intense vertigo symptoms at this point.
- Slowly move your head to the opposite side.
- Turn your body so that it is in line with your head. You will be lying on your side with your head and body facing to the side.
- Sit you upright.

Your provider may need to repeat these steps a few times.

Mastoiditis

Mastoiditis is a serious infection of the mastoid bone at the back of the ear. The infection gets into the airways in the bone.

This is a serious condition that needs medical attention and careful sound therapy once the infection has gone.

Mastoiditis Symptoms

Mastoiditis symptoms may include:

- Fever, irritability, and lethargy
- Swelling of the earlobe
- Redness and tenderness behind the ear
- Drainage from the ear
- Bulging and drooping of the ear

Mastoiditis Complications

Mastoiditis complications may include:

- Facial paralysis
- Nausea, vomiting, vertigo (labyrinthitis)
- Hearing loss
- Brain abscess or meningitis
- Vision changes or headaches (blood clots in the brain)

Useful Websites and contact details

Fit 2 Learn website: https://fit-2-learn.com/

Fit 2 Learn Youtube channel: https://www.youtube.com/@fit2learn657/videos

Fit 2 Learn email: info@fit-2-learn.com

Tomatis Sound Therapy

Tomatis SA: https://www.tomatis.com/en

Forbrain: https://www.forbrain.com/

Pronounce: https://pronounce.com/

Pronounce Youtube channel: https://www.youtube.com/@pronounce_english/videos

Soundsory: https://soundsory.com/

Infinite Headset: https://infinite.tomatis.com/

Primitive Reflex Training

Rhythmic Movement Training International https://rhythmicmovement.org/

RMTI in the UK https://rhythmicmovement.co.uk/

Hear Rate Variance Resources

The Heartmath Institute https://www.heartmath.org/

Rhythm Training and research

Interactive Metronome https://www.interactivemetronome.com/

About the Author

**Charlotte Davies BA Hons, PGCE, NPQH,
Level 4 Tomatis Consultant**

Charlotte is a Director and Founder of Fit 2 Learn CIC, a social enterprise company that combines research and advice to all people on how they can achieve their potential through good control of their own basic physiology. To understand sound therapy, she trained in France with Tomatis TDSA. In 2016 she won the Tomatis Award for best case study.

Charlotte trains people internationally in all aspects of motor-sensory integration. In the UK she works with private individuals and with schools and community organisations to support larger scale screening of children. Charlotte is working on projects with Tomatis.

Charlotte originally trained in Finance, but then moved into teaching when working in the Far East. She left teaching when she could no longer bear to see swathes of young people with correctable barriers to learning being pushed through an education system that was not maximising their skills.

Forbrain®

Speech training tool to
increase language and
attention skills

Soundsory®

Listening and Movement
program to increase balance,
rhythm and coordination

Adaptable to all
levels and ages

Easy to use at home

Only a few minutes a day